D1505746

WESTERN AND CHINESE NEW YEAR'S CELEBRATIONS

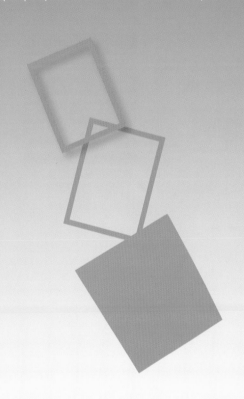

HOLIDAYS AND CELEBRATIONS

Carnival
Christmas and Hanukkah
Easter, Passover, and Other Spring Festivals
Halloween and Commemorations of the Dead
Independence Days
Lent, Yom Kippur, and Other Atonement Days
Ramadan
Religious New Year's Celebrations
Thanksgiving and Other Harvest Festivals
Western and Chinese New Year's Celebrations

WESTERN AND CHINESE NEW YEAR'S CELEBRATIONS

Elizabeth
A. Dice

CHELSEA HOUSE
PUBLISHERS
An imprint of Infobase Publishing

Western and Chinese New Year's Celebrations

Copyright © 2009 by Infobase Publishing

Chelsea House
An imprint of Infobase Publishing
132 West 31st Street
New York, NY 10001

Library of Congress Cataloging-in-Publication Data

Dice, Elizabeth A.
Western and Chinese New Year's celebrations / Elizabeth A. Dice.
    p. cm.—(Holidays and celebrations)
Includes bibliographical references and index.
ISBN 978-1-60413-093-5 (alk. paper)
1. New Year—Juvenile literature. 2. Chinese New Year—Juvenile literature. 3. Calendar—Juvenile literature. I. Title. II. Series.

GT4905.D54 2009
394.2614—dc22

                                                          2008048738

Chelsea House books are available at special discounts when purchased in bulk quantities for businesses, associations, institutions, or sales promotions. Please call our Special Sales Department in New York at (212) 967-8800 or (800) 322-8755.

You can find Chelsea House on the World Wide Web at
http://www.chelseahouse.com

Produced by Print Matters, Inc.
Cover design by Alicia Post

Printed in China

CP PMI 10 9 8 7 6 5 4 3 2 1

This book is printed on acid-free paper.

All links and Web addresses were checked and verified to be correct at the time of publication. Because of the dynamic nature of the Web, some addresses and links may have changed since publication and may no longer be valid.

Contents

Introduction to Holidays and Celebrations.................................... vi

INTRODUCTION
Origins of a Calendar Year 3
Gregorian New Year's Eve/Day (December 31/January 1) 13
Chinese New Year 19

REGIONAL TRADITIONS AND CUSTOMS
Africa...44
Asia..47
Europe..66
Latin America and the Caribbean 79
Middle East 91
North America 92
Oceania 96

Glossary 99
Bibliography 101
Further Resources.. 102
Picture Credits 104
Index 105
About the Author..111

Introduction to Holidays and Celebrations

Holidays mark time. They occupy a space outside of ordinary events and give shape and meaning to our everyday existence. They also remind us of the passage of time as we reflect on Christmases, Passovers, or Ramadans past. Throughout human history, nations and peoples have marked their calendars with special days to celebrate, commemorate, and memorialize. We set aside times to reflect on the past and future, to rest and renew physically and spiritually, and to simply have fun.

In English we call these extraordinary moments "holidays," a contraction of the term "holy day." Sometimes holidays are truly holy days—the Sabbath, Easter, or Eid al-Fitr, for example—but they can also be nonreligious occasions that serve political purposes, address the social needs of communities and individuals, or focus on regional customs and games.

This series explores the meanings and celebrations of holidays across religions and cultures around the world. It groups the holidays into volumes according to theme (such as *Lent, Yom Kippur, and Other Atonement Days; Thanksgiving and Other Harvest Festivals; Independence Days; Easter, Passover, and Other Spring Festivals; Western and Chinese New Year's Celebrations; Religious New Year's Celebrations; Carnival; Ramadan;* and *Halloween and Commemorations of the Dead*) or by their common human experience due to their closeness on the calendar (such as *Christmas and Hanukkah*). Each volume is divided into two sections—the first introduces readers to the origins, history, and common practices associated with the holidays; and the second section takes the reader on a worldwide tour that shows the regional variations and distinctive celebrations within specific countries. The reader will learn how these holidays started, what they mean to the people who celebrate them, and how different cultures celebrate them.

These volumes have an international focus, and thus readers will be able to learn about diversity both at home and throughout the world. We can learn a great deal about a people or nation by the holidays they celebrate. We can also learn from holidays how cultures and religions have interacted and mingled over time. We see in celebrations not just the past through tradition, but the principles and traits that people embrace and value today.

The Chelsea House Holidays and Celebrations series surveys this rich and varied festive terrain. Its 10 volumes show the distinct ways that people all over the world infuse ordinary life with meaning, purpose, or joy. The series cannot be all-inclusive or the last word on so vast a subject, but it offers a vital first step for those eager to learn more about the diverse, fascinating, and vibrant cultures of the world, through the festivities that give expression, order, and meaning to their lives.

A blizzard of confetti snows down in New York's Times Square moments after the New Year begins.

Introduction

No matter where a person lives on Earth, approximately every 365 days one year ends and a new one begins. People all over the world—regardless of race, ethnic background, or religious beliefs—celebrate these two events. In Japan, this time of celebration is called *Shogatsu;* in Mexico, New Year's Day is known as *Año Nuevo;* and in Singapore, many people celebrate both the public New Year's holiday as well as Chinese New Year.

Around the globe, the traditions and celebrations for the last day of one year and the first day of the next have at least one thing in common. Regardless of what calendar is used, these holidays are an opportunity to acknowledge the passing of the old year and to look forward to the year to come. Typically, people reflect on the events of the previous year and set personal and family goals for the next year. Some year-end and new-year traditions are celebrated as public and legal holidays, some as religious holidays (the latter are discussed in the volume called *Religious New Year's Celebrations*), and some as both. It is common for people to serve special good-luck foods and to participate in rituals that symbolize the passing away or ending of the old year and the beginning of a new one. In some countries, New Year is also an occasion for exchanging gifts.

Fireworks are displayed over the Town Hall in Copenhagen, Denmark. Every year crowds gather in the central square to celebrate New Year's Eve and await the last strokes of the Town Hall clock ending the year.

Origins of a Calendar Year

Celebrating the new year is a very old tradition, going back thousands of years. And for thousands of years there have been different ideas as to when the old year ends and a new year begins. Over the centuries, people living in different regions of the world developed their own ways of marking and measuring time, which determined when they considered an old year had ended and a new year had begun.

Seasons for Planting and Harvesting

One thing ancient peoples around the world had in common was a need to know the best times for performing certain tasks. Because they relied on the natural world for food, they watched for signs that would tell them the best times to plant, fish, or gather crops. Even nomadic people (people who travel constantly instead of settling down in one place) kept track of signs that the resources in a particular area might be running out or that the seasons were changing. For example, if the animals they depended on for food migrated (moved from one place or region to another), they followed them.

These early communities were so in tune with the natural world that they first measured time by seasonal changes. In ancient Egypt, for example, they used to recognize three seasons—one when the Nile River flooded, one when the seeds were planted, and a third when the plants

Ancient peoples, who depended on the natural world for food, measured time by changes in the seasons. In ancient Egypt, they recognized three seasons: when the Nile river flooded, when seeds were planted, and when crops were harvested. Here girls pick cotton in a field in the Nile Delta in Egypt, much as their ancestors did.

were harvested. Although basing a year on the changing of the seasons is a solar-based (Sun-based) way to track time, it is not as reliable as following a solar calendar. One reason is that the start and end dates of seasons have always been variable, depending on the location and that year's climate. In addition natural events such as migrations or the date when a particular plant blooms vary from year to year. A community that based the beginning of spring on the arrival of certain migrating birds could not be sure that the birds would migrate on the same day every year.

Within one community or a few communities that shared the same geographical and weather conditions, these seasonal variations in earlier civilizations did not cause much conflict. Practical decisions, such as when they should harvest the corn, did not require precision. In societies in which everyone made decisions together, the group usually shared kinship, that is, everyone in the group was related to someone else within the group. Peace and order were maintained by customs and codes of behavior. Joined together by their identity as a group, each person also shared the same way of looking at time, which made it easy for them to communicate with each other. In other early societies, a leader or leaders were given the job of making decisions that were important to the tribe.

Defining Time by the Phases of the Moon

It is only recently that most people on the planet have been able to own clocks and other mechanical devices for measuring time. In ancient times, people in each region matched their celebrations and rituals to seasonal changes that were important to them. They named divisions of time based on festivals and tasks to be performed. Gradually, however, the idea of defining a specific time period for a year began to take shape. It is likely that the development of a standard calendar was motivated by economic change. When a tribe produced everything it needed, but no more, it did not need to interact extensively with people outside the tribe. Once the group wanted to be able to trade food or objects for something belonging to an outside group, each group needed to be able to express units of time in a way that could be understood by the other. Indeed, much of the early contact between Europeans and Native Americans was motivated by an interest in trade. Similarly, until interstate commerce began in the early republic, localities often kept their own time. In such situations misunderstandings about time could be more than just irritating. They could lead to mistrust, which would be damaging to future relationships between two cultures.

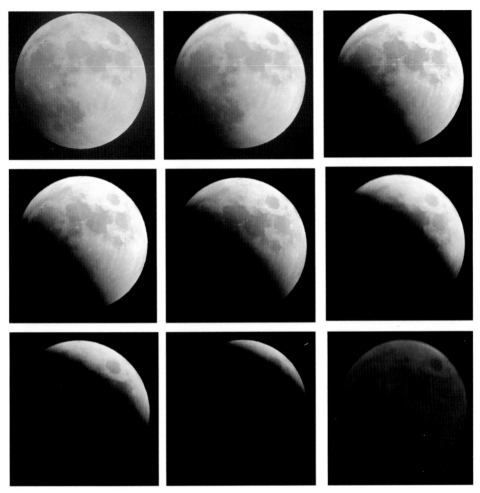

The ancient Sumerians developed the first widely used lunar calendar, based on the phases of the Moon, 4,000 years ago.

In the 21st century B.C.E. the Sumerians (people of the Sumer culture in southern Mesopotamia—the area between the Tigris and the Euphrates Rivers in Asia) were probably responsible for the first widespread use of a lunar calendar, or calendar based on the Moon. The Moon had an easily recognizable cycle of 29 to 30 days, so the Sumerians were one of several peoples that began to divide time by lunar months. Once people began to give names to the cycles of the Moon, the concept of months was born. Most early calendars were in fact just a collection of months.

In the 18th century B.C.E., the Babylonian Empire (also located in southern Mesopotamia, in present-day Iraq) chose to standardize the year and adopted a lunar calendar with the year beginning in early spring.

It was not a perfect calendar, but the lunar calendar noticeably improved communication between people of different backgrounds and cultures.

Great Spirit Moon

The tribes of North American Indians (also known as the First Nations) had their own way of measuring time. Although the tribes did not name individual days or longer time periods, they all recognized days as basic units. Many tribes kept track of days by setting aside a known number of sticks. They would subtract one stick from the bundle for each cycle of night and day that passed until no sticks remained. Like the Sumerians, they counted longer periods of time with moons. The Indians had 12 to 13 moons included in each year. Instead of counting beyond 30 days, they counted the number of times the Moon went from new (or crescent) to full. The cycles of the Moon also became important for religious observances.

There are very few records of calendar-type devices used by the Indians. If they existed, those devices would probably have been considered sacred or secret. Even before the arrival of the colonists, there were different levels of spiritual healers and practitioners in many tribes. Only those who had advanced the furthest in spiritual practices were allowed access to certain objects or information. After the arrival of European settlers, secrecy became survival. As soon as the United States became a nation, there was a push to absorb the Native Americans into white culture and religion, often to the point of persecution or imprisonment. The tribes quickly learned to hide items related to their religious customs, especially once they could be punished for them.

It is known that the Native Peoples divided the year into four, or occasionally five, seasons, but the beginning of a new year varied. Some tribes celebrated the beginning of the year in the fall, others around the time of the spring, or vernal equinox. (This is one of the two days of the year when night is approximately as long as day. The other day is called the autumnal equinox.) Some groups set their own dates for the celebration.

The Calendar Puzzle: Making the Pieces Fit

One might ask, "Why does not everyone use a lunar calendar? The Moon, after all, provides the fundamental calendar unit of a month." The problem has to do with the time it takes the Moon and Earth to complete one revolution. The Moon orbits around Earth in 29.5 days (a lunar month). Twelve lunar months, or a lunar year, equal 354 days,

8 hours, and 53 minutes. However, it takes Earth 365 days, 8 hours, 48 minutes, and 46 seconds to orbit around the Sun. These periods of time do not divide evenly into each other.

What happens if people follow a lunar calendar without trying to correct it to match Earth's orbit around the Sun? The Islamic calendar used by Muslims provides a real-world answer. Muslims are aware of the difference between the solar and lunar calendars, but they have chosen to use the lunar calendar to set the dates for their holy days. As a result, each year the month of Ramadan, which is the ninth month in the Islamic calendar, occurs about 11 days earlier than the previous year. During Ramadan, faithful Muslims do not eat or drink between sunrise and sunset. (Certain groups of people are not required to fast, however, such as the sick, pregnant women, or young children.) If Ramadan falls during the winter, it is not as difficult to fast and go without water because the days are short and cool. Fifteen years later, however, Ramadan will fall during the middle of summer, when the days are long and hot.

In North America, only a few Indian tribes tried to correlate the Moons and years more precisely. The Creek Indians supposedly added a Moon cycle between each pair of years. A tribe of the Dakota, Lakota, and Nakota (formerly known as Sioux) and the Chippewa added a "lost Moon" lunar cycle after 30 Moons had gone by, presumably to solve the difference between the solar and lunar years.

Calendars in Use Around the World Today

There are still several different calendars in use around the world. Some are based on the Sun, some on the Moon, some on both (solilunar calendars), and some on factors that are not related to either.

The five major solar world calendars in use today are the Gregorian, Islamic, Chinese, Jewish, and Hindu calendars. Because the Gregorian and Chinese New Year are the two largest New Year's celebrations in the world, their calendars are examined in greater detail below. What is common among all five of these calendars is that there are seven days in a week and 12 months in a year, but they differ as to when a new day begins. According to the Gregorian (or Western) calendar, a day begins at midnight. In the Islamic calendar, the day begins at sunset. The Chinese define the start of a day at exactly 11:00 P.M. The Jewish calendar day begins at sundown or dusk. For those following the Hindu calendar, the day begins at sunrise or dawn.

Today, there are three different types of calendars in use: lunar, based on the phases of the Moon; solar, based on the movement of the Sun (widely used throughout the Western world); and solilunar, incorporating the movement of both the Moon and the Sun. Here, a full Moon rises in the night sky above the golden domes of the Orthodox Monastery of Caves in Kiev, Ukraine.

There are also major differences as to when a new year begins. The Gregorian calendar simply follows the ancient Roman custom of starting a year on January 1, a tradition dating back to 153 B.C.E. The Islamic calendar follows a different but equally ancient practice of starting a calendar with a specific event: in this case, Muhammad's arrival at Medina from Mecca. The Chinese and Hindu calendars are both based on agricultural cycles. In the Chinese calendar, the new moon preceding the winter solstice opens the year, while the Hindu year begins when the Sun crosses the equator. Different from all of these is the Jewish calendar, which traces the start of its year to biblical instruction. In the book of Exodus, God commands that Nisan be the first calendar month. It is easy to see how the differences between these five calendars can cause confusion within individual countries, let alone across regions of the world.

The Gregorian Calendar

The Gregorian calendar is the one that is most widely used today. It is based on an older calendar known as the Julian calendar. The Julian calendar is named after Julius Caesar, the military leader and dictator of ancient Rome, who introduced it in 46 B.C.E. The Julian calendar has 365 days divided into 12 months and begins on January 1. This date was chosen due to political pressures within the Roman Republic. The new year originally began in the middle of March; however, various circumstances forced officers to take their posts earlier in the year. In 153 B.C.E., they changed the calendar to suit their needs and the tradition remained. An extra day, or leap day, is added every four years (February 29) so that the years will average out to 365.242, which is quite close to the actual 365.242199 days of Earth's orbit.

Caesar adopted the Julian calendar on the advice of the Greek astronomer Sosigenes, who had unintentionally overestimated the length of the year by 11 minutes and 14 seconds. These 11 minutes and 14 seconds may not sound like very much, but they add up year by year. By 1582, the Julian calendar had shifted the dates of the seasons by about 10 days. As a result, the calendar would show the longest day of the year taking place about 10 days after it actually happened. Pope Gregory XIII proclaimed a new calendar in 1582 to fix the error, and thus the Gregorian calendar was born. It was quickly adopted in Italy, Spain, Portugal, and the states within Germany that were Catholic. Other nations gradually began to use it as well: Protestant states in Germany in 1699, England and its colonies in 1752, Sweden in 1752, Japan in 1873, China in 1912, the Soviet Union in 1918, and Greece in 1923. Countries that are primarily Muslim continue to use the lunar Islamic calendar.

Today commerce and communications tie the people of the world together as never before. As a result, non-Western countries that have their own calendar system (not the Gregorian one) often use the Gregorian calendar for banking and other business transactions. This is especially true when computers are involved. These countries may observe December 31 and January 1 as public holidays, but the religious or ethnic New Year is often the celebration more important to the people.

Among the New Year's observances based on religious, rather than civic, calendars are Rosh Hashanah, the somber and very holy Jewish New Year; Diwali, the Hindu "Festival of Lights"; and El am Hejir, the Islamic New Year that marks the exodus of Muhammad. These are often known as movable holidays because they occur on different days every year in

A Web Site for Converting Calendar Dates

John Walker, an American computer programmer now living in Switzerland, has created a public-domain Web site that allows people to input dates in one calendar to see the equivalent dates in another calendar. In addition to the more well-known calendars such as the Gregorian, Julian, Islamic, Jewish, and Indian calendars, Walker includes calendars such as the Mayan calendar and the French Republican calendar. (French emperor Napoleon Bonaparte abolished the French Republican calendar effective January 1, 1806, a little more than 12 years after it was introduced, which is why it is unfamiliar to most people.)

relation to the Gregorian calendar. In fact, sometimes a holiday that is a yearly holiday in terms of the ethnic group that celebrates it can take place twice within the year based on the Gregorian calendar. Sometimes just the opposite is true—a full Gregorian year may go by without a religious new year occurring.

One of the most unusual ethnic calendars is the Mayan calendar, which is actually a series of calendars and almanacs introduced at least as far back as the sixth century B.C.E. (The Maya are the indigenous peoples of Mexico, Guatemala, and Belize.) Scientists who have studied the Mayan calendar have determined that the ancient Maya were thinking in terms of millennia, or thousands, of years long before the Europeans did so. In the Mayan system, the calendars can interlock and be moved together, which allows for additional cycles to be generated from the movement of the parts. It follows a 260-day cycle, so the date for New Year's Eve in relation to the Gregorian calendar changes from year to year. This calendar system was used by the Mayan civilization before its second collapse in the 16th century and is still used by some Mayan groups in the highlands of Guatemala today. It is also enjoying revived interest as groups of Maya in other regions have begun to celebrate their culture.

Similar indigenous groups lived in essentially every country of Latin America before the arrival of Europeans. Though some groups disappeared after the arrival of outsiders, many have not. After years of being used as laborers, enduring little or no political representation and encountering prejudice from a majority that does not understand their language or culture, the indigenous people of Latin America are finding a new sense of identity. Along with this new sense of identity comes a renewed interest in celebrating New Year according to their culture's calendar, rather than the Gregorian calendar. The more elaborate celebrations take place in urban areas, while in the rural villages and towns informality marks the New Year's celebrations.

Chinese Calendar

The Chinese calendar is a lunar-based calendar that dates back to about 2600 B.C.E. Over time it has come to incorporate elements of the solar calendar, but its months and new year are still based on the position of the Moon. According to Chinese astrology, each year is named after one of

Children dressed in mouse costumes perform at Beijing's Temple of the Earth on the eve of Chinese New Year. The children are dressed as mice to celebrate the Year of the Rat. Temples in Beijing hold fairs to celebrate the Spring Festival, which marks the beginning of the Lunar New Year.

Some Famous People Born in the Year of the Rat

Some famous "rats" are actors Samuel L. Jackson, Gwyneth Paltrow, Reiko Aylesworth, Scarlett Johansson, Sean Penn, and America Ferrera; musicians Wolfgang Amadeus Mozart, Louis Armstrong, and Bono; artists Claude Monet and Toulouse-Lautrec; athletes Shaquille O'Neal, Zinedine Zidane, and Sasha Cohen; Nobel-prize-winning physicist Steven Chu; and leaders George Washington, Prince Charles, and Al Gore.

12 animals. The animals vary slightly from country to country. In China the animals are rat, ox, tiger, rabbit, dragon, snake, horse, sheep, monkey, rooster, dog, and pig. Each of these represents a sign in the Chinese zodiac. There are no constellations corresponding to these animals as there are in the Western zodiac, and in certain countries some minor changes occur. In Vietnam, the water buffalo replaces the ox, the cat is used instead of the rabbit, and the goat is swapped for the sheep. The Japanese use the boar instead of the pig, and Thais use the Naga instead of the dragon. (Naga is a serpent-god that resembles a cobra.) The names of the animals repeat continually, which is why someone born in 1998 and someone born in 2010 will both be born in the Year of the Tiger.

According to Chinese tradition, people's personalities are influenced by the year in which they are born. The year 2008 in the Gregorian calendar corresponds to the Chinese year 4705-4706, and is the Year of the Rat. In Western countries, the rat is not an animal people would want to be associated with, but in Asia, rats are seen differently. In both China and Japan, rats are symbols of good luck and wealth. For example, people born in the Year of the Rat are supposed to be good at finding sources of money and holding onto them. Society's pioneers and leaders are said to number an especially high proportion of "rats." They are also believed to be charming but practical, and willing to work hard in pursuit of what they care about most.

Gregorian New Year's Eve/Day (December 31/January 1)

Whatever the customs and in whatever language one says "Happy New Year," the two-day public holiday is probably the most widely celebrated holiday in the world. New Year's Eve and New Year's Day are celebrated as public, or civic, holidays in virtually every part of the globe. In general, businesses, banks, and schools are closed on New Year's Day. The majority of the world uses this time to share and celebrate with friends and family. People attempt to make amends for the previous year's transgressions. They often resolve to reform certain aspects of their lives, using

In Ecuador, a child walks by figures representing television characters. Ecuadoreans traditionally practice the "Old Year's Burn," when a puppet or figure, representing the past year, is burned at the last minute of December 31 to enter the new year with a clean slate.

the new year as a symbolic opportunity to make a fresh start. On New Year's Eve people gather together to count down the hours, minutes, and eventually seconds before the new year begins. In the various time zones around the world, the stroke of midnight is a special moment that may be accompanied by toasts, short speeches, and the exchange of good wishes for a prosperous new year. New Year's Day often features parades and other communal celebrations. These can be as large as citywide festivals or as small as meals shared among family and friends.

Origins and History

New Year is the oldest continually celebrated holiday in the world, dating back to the ancient Babylonians of 2000 B.C.E. Their new year began in spring, as it was the time when they planted crops for the forthcoming year. At this time they held an 11-day celebration to commemorate the start of the harvest cycle. Such festivities were common practice throughout the world in ancient times, as early civilizations based their calendars on the movements of the Sun and Moon and the rituals of agriculture. The Egyptians and Persians celebrated the new year during the spring equi-

New Year's Eve revelers react as confetti is released in New York's Times Square.

People toast during New Year's celebrations in Moscow's Red Square. Each year thousands of people gather in and around Red Square to mark the new year by listening to the Kremlin's bells and watching fireworks.

nox in what is present-day March, while the Greeks used the winter solstice.

With the introduction of the Julian calendar, January 1 was established as the first day of the new year. *January* originally meant the "Month of Janus," named after a Roman god with two faces: One of his faces looks forward, into the future; the other looks backward, into the past. Janus is associated with beginnings and endings. He is the guardian of gates and doors, and as such his name was chosen to name January as the gateway to the year. January 1 was not immediately adopted as New Year's Day, however, as countries wrestled with the predominance of church calendars, local custom, and alternative methods of timekeeping. By the 16th century January 1 became more widely accepted, beginning with the Republic of Venice in 1522. Sweden, France, and other countries followed suit, and by the 18th century the date was standardized. Thailand was the last country to adopt the date, doing so in 1941.

Customs

The worldwide recognition of January 1 as the date for the new year led to the development of common themes and celebrations across many nationalities. Some of these, such as making resolutions (setting goals) for the upcoming year, rekindling friendships, and returning borrowed items, were traditional practices stretching back to Babylonian times. Over the years these archaic customs were modified to include things such as gift-giving and sharing meals. As transportation improved and people were able to traverse greater distances, neighboring villages and towns could celebrate the new year together. This led to a greater exchange of local traditions and, eventually, larger-scale celebrations such as concerts, dances, and festivals. Even as the holiday has grown in scope, the focus has always remained the same: New Year is as an opportunity to come together, evaluate the past year, and prepare for the months ahead.

For hundreds of years New Year's Day was the focus of the holiday. By the early 20th century, however, the emphasis was placed on New Year's Eve. With the refinement of the International Date Line (an imaginary line extending between the North Pole and the South Pole, which marks off one calendar day from the next with a time difference of 24 hours on either side) and the division of the world into various time zones in 1884, people everywhere could share in the passage of one year to the next. Though it was not broadcast on television, radio, and the Internet as it is today, the stroke of midnight nonetheless became the definitive New Year's experience. This continues today, as celebrants gather together to count down the seconds until January 1, make toasts, and watch fireworks displays in person or on live television. In the modern era people

Some New Year's Traditions

Depending on where people live, one or more of the following New Year's traditions may be familiar:

- Images of Father Time and Baby New Year
- Singing "Auld Lang Syne"
- Watching the New Year's ball drop in New York City's Times Square
- Eating 12 grapes as a wish for 12 good months to come
- Watching spectacular, noisy fireworks displays
- Watching a parade on TV or in person
- Hearing the Buddhist temple bells strike 108 times
- Eating Hoppin' John (a good-luck dish from the American South made of ham and black-eyed peas)
- Making New Year's resolutions
- Giving gifts of coal to feed a fire or shortbread to feed the senses

A Filipino boy sells horns in Manila, Philippines, for the New Year's celebrations on December 31. Many Filipinos celebrate the New Year with firecrackers and other noisemakers in the belief that the noise will drive away bad luck and evil spirits.

are able to see live satellite feeds of celebrations all over the world as they occur, thus bringing once-distant nations together for a brief moment of shared joy. Newspapers and magazines mark the end of the year with "Year-in-Review" editions that survey the events of the past 12 months. These publications sum up the social, political, and cultural movements of the year and point the way for the changes to come.

New Year's Greetings
Around the World

In many countries, people exchange New Year's greetings:

Afrikaans	Voorspoedige Nuwe Jaar
Arabic	Kul 'am wa antum bikhair
Basque	Urte berri on
Bengali	Shuvo Noboborsho
Chinese (Cantonese)	Sun nien fai lok
Chinese (Mandarin)	Xin nian hao
Czech	Stastny Novy Rok
Danish	Godt nytår
Dutch	Gelukkig nieuwjaar
English	Happy New Year
Esperanto	Bonan Novjaron
Finnish	Onnellista uutta vuotta
French	Bonne année
German	Ein glückliches neues Jahr
Greek	Eutychismenos o kainourgios chronos
Hawaiian	Hauoli Makahiki hou
Hebrew	Shana Tova
Hungarian	Boldog uj evet
Indonesian (Bahasa)	Selamat Tahun Baru
Italian	Felice anno nuovo *or* buon anno
Japanese	Akemashite Omedetou Gozaimasu
Korean	Sehe Bokmanee Bateuseyo
Laotian (Hmong)	Nyob Zoo Xyoo Tshiab
Latin	Felix sit annus novus
Nigerian (Hausa)	Barka da sabuwar shekara
Norwegian	Godt Nytt År
Philippines (Tagalog)	Manigong Bagong Taon
Polish	Szczęśliwego Nowego Roku
Romanian	La Multi Ani Si Un An Nou Fericit
Russian	S Novym Godom
Samoan	La manuia le Tausaga Fou
Spanish	Feliz año nuevo
Swahili	Heri za Mwaka Mpya
Swedish	Gott nytt ar
Vietnamese	Chuc mung nam moi
Welsh	Blwyddyn Newydd Dda

Chinese New Year

Every year, more than a billion people celebrate the holiday of Chinese New Year. Other names for the Chinese New Year are the Lunar New Year and the Spring Festival (Chun Jie). The holiday begins on the second new Moon after the winter solstice (the day the Sun is at its greatest distance from the equator, creating the shortest day of the year). This means that it falls sometime between January 21 and February 19 on the Gregorian calendar. In many places the festivities end 15 days later on a full Moon, making Chinese New Year the longest of Chinese holidays. Chinese New Year is officially celebrated in Brunei, China, Fiji, Hong Kong, Indonesia, Macau, Malaysia, Mauritius, Singapore, Taiwan, and Thailand. The festival has also become popular wherever Chinese people live. Because there are people of Chinese descent throughout the world, there are also special Chinese New Year's celebrations held every year around the globe in cities such as New York; San Francisco; Vancouver, Canada; Lima, Peru; Paris, France; Melbourne, Australia; and even Butte, Montana.

For some countries, this is the most important New Year's celebration. Regardless of where they are, people throughout the world will greet each other on the first day of Chinese New Year by saying either *"Xin nian hao*!" in Mandarin or *"Sun nien fai lok*!" in Cantonese (both mean "Happy New Year!")

Origins

The exact origins of Chinese New Year are unknown. Centuries ago, about the only time that farmers had to rest was after a harvest and before the next spring planting. In ancient China, celebrating the harvest coincided with the beginning of the new year on the lunar calendar. As people came together to socialize, they brought food they had accumulated through fishing, hunting, or farming. They ate together, danced, and sang. This was a time for family reunions, even though family members usually lived closer together than they do in current-day China. It was also a time to leave behind the mistakes of the past and begin life anew on New Year's Day.

The Role of Buddhism, Daoism, and Confucianism in Chinese New Year

Buddhism and Daoism

The majority of the Chinese people follow the religions of Buddhism or Daoism or both. However, many followers of these religions consider them philosophies, or spiritual and moral ways of living one's life, rather than religions because they do not teach the idea of a divine creator. In Buddhist and Daoist homes, altars and statues are cleaned thoroughly as part of the New Year's preparation, and new decorations are placed on the altars.

Buddhism is based on the teachings of its founder, Siddhartha Gautama (about 560–480 B.C.E.). However all forms of Buddhism acknowledge the possibility of more than one buddha ("awakened" or "enlightened one"), so Siddhartha Gautama is sometimes called Gautama Buddha, to set him apart from the others.

There are many varieties of Buddhism, and for most there is great emphasis on discipline and technique in mastering perceptions, thoughts, and even the body. The different schools of thought share in recognizing the principle, as Gautama Buddha taught, that each person is responsible for his or her own enlightenment:

My teaching is not a philosophy. It is the result of direct experience. . . .
My teaching is a means of practice, not something to hold onto or worship.
My teaching is like a raft used to cross the river. Only a fool would carry
the raft around after he had already reached the other shore of liberation.

(Thich Nhat Hanh 1991)

Followers of Buddhism refrain from eating meat on the first and seventh days of the New Year's celebrations. They also usually go to the local temple and perform chants and prayers, as well as burn incense. For Buddhists, burning incense is a way of sending messages of gratitude through fragrance. It also is a way to purify oneself and to share with others.

Daoism is often defined as a set of universal beliefs. One fundamental belief of Daoism is that the world is composed of opposites such as up and down, open and shut, strong and weak. One cannot exist without the other; for example, light has little meaning without darkness. The most essential pair of opposites is yin and yang. According to the Chinese, yin

(Moon) is a creative force, associated with attributes such as feminine, cold, receptive, and dark, whereas yang (Sun) is a dynamic force whose attributes include masculine, heat, active, and light. The symbol for these two forces is recognizable even in Western countries because it often appears on signs for martial art studios, book covers, jewelry designs, and in any other graphic related to Chinese philosophy. The symbol consists of a black shape, something like a tadpole, curved around an identical, but oppositely situated white shape. Within the widest part of the white shape there is a black circle, and in the widest part of the black shape, a white circle. The two shapes fit together perfectly to form a larger circle, which represents balance between the two forces. Such visual themes are especially poignant during the Chinese New Year, with its focus on reconciling earthly and heavenly duties. For instance, on the ninth day of the new year believers honor their living family members with prayers to the Jade Emperor of the Daoist pantheon. The Jade Emperor is known as the ruler of all realms below heaven, including that of humans. Prayers to him thus link up the natural world with the divine.

The book *Daodejing* (also known as *Tao-te Ching* and *Tao te Ching*) attempts to put Daoist beliefs in written form and is therefore considered an essential text for understanding Daoism. *Daodejing* is a short book of 81 texts or verses, believed to have been authored by a Chinese scholar from the sixth century B.C.E. named Laozi (Lao Tzu). There are numerous translations of the book from Chinese into English. One version by Gia-Fu Feng and Jane English combines the text of the English translation opposite black and white photographs overlaid with the graceful brushwork of the Chinese characters. Here is one verse from their translation, which provides a glimpse of Daoist philosophy:

Knowledge
Knowing others is wisdom;
Knowing the self is enlightenment.
Mastering others requires force;
Mastering the self requires strength;
He who knows he has enough is rich.
Perseverance is a sign of willpower.
He who stays where he is endures.
To die but not to perish is to be eternally present.

(Lao Tsu 1972)

Confucianism and Ancestor Worship

Since the time of the sixth century B.C.E., the principles of the Chinese philosopher Confucius—respect for parents and elders, and the importance of family—has lain at the heart of Chinese culture.

Chinese New Year's celebrations revolve around living family members, but many participants also perform ceremonies to honor family members who are deceased. They believe that their ancestors, the relatives who preceded them, remain with them in some way, even after death.

While it is customary to honor one's ancestors throughout the year, during holidays such as Chinese New Year it is especially important to show one's love and respect for them by burning incense and making food offerings. The belief is that ancestors can help make the coming year a good one, or might be able to give advice on difficult matters. The Chinese hold the opinion that they will be prosperous and happy if their ancestors are prosperous and happy.

History

Although China has often had a violent past, it has never been ruled by another country with the exception of some provinces and special administrative regions (SARs). The influence and rule of China was even greater in earlier centuries than it is now. At one time the modern-day countries of Vietnam, Laos, Cambodia, Myanmar, Korea, and Taiwan were all part of Chinese empires. Chinese New Year has influenced the New Year's celebrations in all of these countries, as well as China's geographic neighbors Nepal, Bhutan, and Mongolia.

Chinese history goes back more than 4,000 years. Today China is divided into provinces. Most inhabitants identify themselves with the province or region in which they live or in which they were born. While the central government administers all 28 of the geographical divisions, five have more constitutional rights than the other 23, so they are known as autonomous, or independent, regions. Each one of these independent regions is home to a specific ethnic minority, such as Tibetans or Mongols. While the other provinces have governors, the autonomous regions each have a chairman, and the chairman must be a member of the ethnic minority.

In addition China has four metropolitan areas called municipalities that are so large they are treated like provinces. Shanghai and Beijing are the most well-known of these. There are also two SARs. These regions have even more independence than the autonomous provinces. The first one—Hong Kong—was transferred to the Republic of China by the United Kingdom in 1997. Portugal similarly transferred Macau two years later.

One area that is still being disputed is Taiwan. Taiwan has been considered China's 23rd province since the People's Republic of China (known also by the abbreviation "PRC") was established in 1949. However, Taiwan is controlled by the political body known as the Republic of China (known too by its abbreviation, "ROC"). The debate is whether the island of Taiwan and the smaller nearby islands are part of the People's Republic of China or independent. If the ROC declares Taiwan independent, the PRC has said it will take military action against it. The people who live in Taiwan and the accompanying islands have mixed views on the issue. Some wish to reunite with China sometime in the future, others want to separate, and still others want things to stay as they are, with Taiwan having some political control without breaking away completely from mainland China.

When the Chicken Talks to the Duck: Cantonese and Mandarin Dialects

There are many dialects of Chinese. Two of the most common are Cantonese and Mandarin. Mandarin is the official language of mainland China and Taiwan. It is used by most Chinese schools, colleges, and universities, as well as on television, the radio, and in most movies. Mandarin is also one of the five official languages of the United Nations. Cantonese is the dialect spoken in the province of Guandong, the autonomous region of Guangxi, and in the majority of Chinese communities in Europe, Australia, North America, and other parts of the world. As more people have migrated from Taiwan and the northern provinces of China, the number of Mandarin-speaking people outside of China has been growing rapidly. In developed communities of Chinese immigrants, such as California's San Francisco Bay area, there are television and radio channels that feature Mandarin and others that broadcast only in Cantonese.

People who speak only Mandarin or only Cantonese cannot understand each other. In Hong Kong, there is a joke that this is like "the chicken talking to the duck." Both languages are tonal, that is different tones change the meaning of the same sound. Mandarin has four tones, and Cantonese has six primary and numerous secondary tones. The two

Mandarin and Cantonese Dialects

If a person decides to study Chinese, there are two main dialects to chose from: Mandarin and Cantonese. Which one to learn depends on how the language will be used. If someone plans to research acupuncture or Traditional Chinese Medicine (TCM), Mandarin is a better choice since most of the acupuncture points and herbs are in pinyin—the system of writing out sounds of standard Mandarin in the Roman (or Latin) alphabet that is used for English. Mandarin would also allow a person to be understood in Hong Kong, Macau, and Guangzhou (formerly called Canton). On the other hand, Cantonese is the "mother tongue" of Hong Kong, where it is used every day for conversations between family, friends, and for talking to people in shops, taxis, or restaurants. It is also the preferred dialect of many business people in southeast China and Southeast Asia, although English is gaining ground as the language of business.

dialects have different vowels and consonants as well. Speakers of the two dialects can only understand each other if they communicate by writing, because they use the same written characters with minimal exceptions. Still, it can be hard for someone who knows Mandarin to read Cantonese since it often contains a lot of figures of speech that are unfamiliar to Mandarin speakers.

A New Kind of Chinese New Year

China has always been home to a wide variety of religious beliefs. However, when civil war in China ended in 1949, the Communist Party established the People's Republic of China and banned the practice of any religion. The party viewed it as backward and superstitious. It also associated religion, particularly Christianity, with countries that rejected communism, such as the United States.

Instead of eliminating celebration of Chinese New Year, the Communist Party of China (CCP) shaped it for its own purposes. The "folk" aspects of the holiday—housecleaning, repainting rooms, purchasing new clothing, haircutting—were emphasized and the spiritual side of the holiday was ignored or repressed. For example, the communists prohibited the production and distribution of traditional *nian hua*, posters created specifically for Chinese New Year showing idealized babies and symbols and motifs representing luck and prosperity. Instead the party had their own artists create images they called "new *nian hua*" to use as propaganda, that is, they had posters produced that would specifically express their political ideas.

Rise of the Red Guard

Seventeen years after the establishment of the People's Republic of China and the banning of religious practice, political events in China took a different turn. In 1966, the chairman of the CCP, Mao Zedong, began what would be a 10-year revolution (later referred to as the Cultural Revolution) by gathering together a group of radical followers. This group undermined the other communist leaders by accusing them of losing their "revolutionary" spirit, and of adopting "bourgeois," or middle-class values.

Mao believed that in order to have a true revolution, traditional Chinese culture had to be destroyed. Beliefs that are central to the celebration of Chinese New Year—reverence for ancestors, belief in gods and spirits, the honoring of spiritual figures such as Buddha, the traditional family structure, and respect for elders—were all targeted by Mao and his followers. Mao closed schools and persuaded students from the cities to form a youth army known as the Red Guard. He then riled up the Red Guard and persuaded them to verbally attack officials, intellectuals, and older people in power. Many people died during the Cultural Revolution.

Chinese music and even ancient Chinese instruments, some with as much as 3,000 years of history behind them, were criticized as symbols of Chinese high culture, because they were usually only available to members of the upper class. Under Mao's instructions, they were gathered up and locked away, left to grow brittle with age and riddled with insect holes.

In fact, all forms of artistic expression were rigidly controlled by Mao's government. As a result, Chinese New Year became a pale ghost of its former self. Rural areas were less affected by the Cultural Revolution, since they were home to the peasants Mao considered the model for the rest of society. In the cities and larger towns, however, both everyday life and holidays became radically different.

Mao also destroyed many places of worship such as temples, mosques, and churches. Other religious buildings were converted to nonreligious buildings. In this environment, celebrating the religious, spiritual, and familial aspects of Chinese New Year was expressly forbidden.

The death of Mao and Prime Minister Zhou Enlai in 1976 was followed by a power struggle in which the Maoists were dislodged by the moderates led by Deng Xiaoping. During the next decade there was improvement in agricultural and economic policies.

In 1989 there was a massive pro-democracy student demonstration in Tiananmen Square in Beijing. After a several-week long sit-in, Chinese government troops opened fire killing many peaceful protesters. The incident drew international condemnation. People around the world demonstrated for reform in China. Chinese officials knew that these demonstrators, and others who might share pro-reform sentiments, were also consumers of Chinese goods. China needed these consumers for its thriving economy and its citizens were becoming more prosperous and insistent on fundamental liberties. Official toleration and acceptance of many traditions based on religion grew. By the time of the 2008 Summer Olympics in Beijing, China proudly presented a diverse, socially open society. Though political dissent is still not easily accommodated, the opening with respect to long-established customs that were oppressed during the Mao years remains. In 2008 the government shifted the official start date of the three-day Chinese New Year holiday to begin a day earlier to make travel easier for workers returning home.

Red for Good Luck

The color red repels evil spirits and brings good fortune, so the windows and doors receive fresh coats of red paint in preparation for New Year's. Even the doors and window frames of houses are believed to influence a family's luck. People avoid wearing black or white at this time because those are colors that they associate with mourning and funerals. On a personal level the Chinese try to pay off their debts so they can face the coming year with a clean slate. People are also encouraged to make apologies or end grudges. Since it is considered important to end the year on a positive note, this is a good time to thank coworkers or employees for their hard work.

Customs

Making a Clean Sweep for the New Year

Preparations begin long before Chinese New Year arrives. People spend much of the last month of the lunar year getting ready for the holiday. They thoroughly clean their homes, making sure that every part of the house is fresh and in order so that no bad luck might be left from the year that is ending. (This is similar to the American tradition of "spring cleaning," during which homes are cleaned and aired out in preparation for the new season. It also resembles the Jewish tradition of thoroughly cleaning the home before Passover—especially to remove any trace of bread, which is not eaten for the holiday.) The clean-up applies to more than just the home. Cities and towns use this time to sponsor clean-ups of public areas such as parks and squares.

Special Poems for the New Year

One custom belonging to Chinese New Year's is to hang up poems about spring or wishes of good fortune for the coming year. These messages are called *hui chun*, which means "returning to spring" or "recovering," or *chun lian* ("spring couplet"). The characters are written vertically, in black ink on long pieces of red paper. One explanation of this custom is based on a legend that about 2,000 years ago there were two brothers who were skilled at catching ghosts. It became a custom to paste pictures of the brothers in doorways to scare away evil spirits. Over time, couplets in Chinese replaced pictures of the brothers.

Some common messages contained in the poems might be "Heaven adds another year of time and people add another year of life," or "May the star of happiness, the star of wealth, and the star of long life shine on you."

For calligraphers, the couplets are works of art. Chang Ping-huang, president of the Republic of China (Taiwan) Calligraphy Association says: "When I write a word, I am bringing it to life . . . the words themselves must be written in a generous and happy way—not with thin lines or a severe style—since everyone who enters the house will be affected." (Logan n.d.) Although Chang can receive as much as the equivalent of $3,000 dollars for a pair of couplets, he and the Calligraphy Association often distribute their work for free, so that everyone can share this ancient tradition.

Another explanation for the couplets comes from a legend that explains several other New Year's traditions, such as the use of firecrackers. There are many variations of the legend, but in all of them the central character is a cruel, man-eating monster named Nian. Sometimes Nian is described as having a long tail and a horn on his head, but in other descriptions, he has a lion-like head and a body that resembles an elephant. In most accounts he has a gigantic mouth that allows him to eat several people in one bite. In ancient China, he supposedly came down from the mountains (or in some versions, out of the sea) and terrorized villages. An old man told the people to set off firecrackers, beat drums, and burn bamboo to frighten the beast away. The plan worked! As a result, to this day the Chinese customarily beat gongs and drums, light firecrackers, and decorate their houses with red to drive away monsters.

Cut Paper Decorations and Posters

In addition to calligraphed couplets, elaborate paper cut-outs (also called paper cuts) are popular decorations for Chinese New Year. After folding the paper several times, the artists often use scissors, razor knives, and hole punchers to create designs that are so delicate there is just enough paper to hold them together. Some are even three-dimensional.

New Year's Puns

The paper cut-outs, like other New Year's traditions, often involve puns or homonyms—words that have the same sound as another word. The homonyms and puns are playful ways of suggesting prosperity or good luck without stating it directly. For example, the Mandarin Chinese pronunciation of the word for "bat" sounds like the character for good fortune, so cut-outs of bats often show up in decorations. Other images such as fish, the animals of the Chinese zodiac, or the God of Wealth are also popular.

During New Year the Chinese character *fu* (happiness) appears on banners, red envelopes, and posters, often upside-down. The pronunciation of "upside-down" in Chinese is a homologue for (or, sounds the same as) "comes" or "arrives," so the sign really means: "Happiness comes (to your household)," or to whoever looks at the poster.

Chubby Babies

At New Year people hang up a special kind of colorful poster, especially in the rural parts of northern China. These posters feature one or more smiling, chubby Chinese babies. The pictures are called *nian hua* and are specifically created for this holiday. *Nian hua* posters have existed for hundreds of years as a type of folk art and symbol of luck, so the subject of the paintings has varied with the times. During the long history of *nian hua*, politics have even sometimes played a role in determining the subject matter the artist paints.

The babies in the current *nian hua* posters are idealized, intentionally painted to look perfect instead of like real children. In almost every poster a happy, pink-cheeked baby rides or frolics with a giant carp (a type of fish) painted red. Often the babies are surrounded by brightly painted flowers such as peonies, peach blossoms, or lotuses. These flowers have positive meanings for the Chinese, such as long life, abundance,

From Gods and Heroes to Roly-poly Babies

The earliest *nian hua* probably featured gods or heroes, but roly-poly babies have been popular since at least the 1930s. Posters from this era still show up in galleries and on the Internet as collectors' items.

Prosperity Cake for Chinese New Year

Fa gao, which means "prosperity cake," is a favorite food for Chinese New Year. The cake is made from wheat flour, water, and sugar, with yeast or baking powder added to make the cake rise. The cake is steamed until its top splits open. It symbolizes good fortune rising up and spilling over during the new year.

and beauty. Generally, the artists seem to cram into each picture as many symbols and motifs representing luck or prosperity as they can: coins, pastries, Chinese characters, mandarin ducks, trees covered with perfect fruit or blossoms, and buckets of fruit including huge kumquats, glistening peaches, oranges, or tangerines.

Lucky Foods

In addition to cleaning and decorating, there is much baking and cooking done to prepare for a new year. Special dishes are prepared ahead of time. During the celebrations, meals are made and eaten according to which day of the holiday it is. Many of the foods served have names related to hopes for the coming year. For example, a common dinner includes seafood and dumplings. Both dishes represent good wishes. The Cantonese word for lettuce, *saang choy*, sounds like "rising fortune." Consequently, lettuce wraps often appear at New Year's meals.

On the last day before the Chinese New Year, everyone

A man shops for Chinese New Year's decorations at a shop in Hong Kong.

cooks enough food for two days. This is done so that all knives, scissors, and other sharp tools can be stored away. Nothing sharp should be left out because it might "cut" the family's good fortune.

Fish is another common food served at New Year. In particular, a steamed whole fish symbolizes good luck and a long life for those who eat it. The Chinese word for fish is *yu*. This word sounds a lot like the Chinese word that means *surplus,* or plenty. Therefore, a common New Year's greeting is to wish others a surplus of good fortune in the year to come. It is also common to hang decorations with fish images to express wishes for abundance.

Round is Good

Round foods are especially popular during New Year because they suggest completion, wholeness, round coins, and the shape of the full Moon. Other foods associated with good fortune are oysters, prawns, and mandarin oranges. In the Cantonese dialect of Chinese, the name for these sweet oranges also means "gold." Baked goods that have seeds

Chinese New Year Cards

Chinese New Year's cards have become increasingly popular in the United States. Hallmark introduced Chinese New Year's cards in 1999, and in 2004, San Francisco graphic designer Grace Wu created her own business called New Year Designs. She began with designs for the Year of the Monkey, but now she produces 11 different animal characters and sells more than 50 designs. There are also several Web sites that feature free, animated Chinese New Year's e-cards with accompanying music. Typically, the designs are splashed with bold colors, especially red, to repel evil spirits and bring good fortune, and the text is in Chinese as well as English. Chinese motifs usually decorate the cards with images such as coins, flowers, dragons, lanterns, and flying cranes. Most of these motifs symbolize strength and prosperity for the new year. The zodiac animal for the year is featured in many of the designs, so for 2008 grinning cartoon rats wave from the cards. In 2009, oxen will be in the spotlight.

Baked sweet sesame seed balls, a traditional Chinese New Year's food, are displayed at a store in Hong Kong.

in them, such as sweet sesame seed balls (*jien duy*), are often served during New Year's celebrations. The round shape and gold color symbolize prosperity, especially because as the balls are fried, they increase several times in size. For Chinese New Year, this is a happy metaphor, or comparison, between the food and the idea of a small investment growing and bringing back a large return. *Jien duy* are traditionally filled with a bit of sweet red bean paste, making them like a Chinese version of jelly doughnuts in the United States.

Boiled dumplings, another traditional New Year's dish, have a slightly different meaning. The dumplings symbolize good wishes for the family, but especially in terms of having more sons. In China, there is a tradition of preferring sons, particularly in rural areas, because they can do more farm work, help support their parents when they are elderly, and inherit the family

Superstitions Related to Making New Year's Dumplings

There are certain superstitions related to making the dumplings for New Year. It is believed that any bad feelings between family members should be resolved before the dumplings are cooked. Supposedly if anyone says something unpleasant, an evil spirit will steal the dumplings. It is also believed that it is best not to count the dumplings while making them because doing so will lead to scarcity in the year to come. It is also bad luck if a dumpling breaks apart while it is being cooked. It means that difficulties will arise in the upcoming year.

The Chinese New Year Storm of 2008

In 2008, unusually severe winter storms hit China at the worst possible time—just as everyone was traveling to visit their relatives for Chinese New Year on February 7. Ice and heavy snows left more than 100,000 people stranded in train stations, brought down power lines, and flattened crops. The brutal conditions also interrupted shipments of fresh food, oil, and gas. Some areas in China experienced the worst snowfalls seen in decades, which not only halted the trains but made the roads impassable, especially in eastern China. In the southern town of Guangzhou, authorities had to set up temporary shelters for passengers who had been stuck at the train station. China's railway authority sent out 22,046 pounds of rice, vegetables, and meat, plus 20,000 boxes of instant noodles and drinking water to provide for the stranded passengers. Many regions had power outages. The central government took urgent measures to resolve the problem. Chinese Premier Wen Jibao announced, "Urgently mobilize and work as one to wage this tough battle against disaster. . . Ensure that the people enjoy a joyful and auspicious Spring Festival [an alternative name the Chinese give the holiday]." (Buckley 2008)

name and land. When the Chinese government realized that the population was growing at an excessive rate, it began to ask parents to voluntarily limit the number of children they had. In 1979 it went even further, passing laws that limited a family to one child. As a result, many Chinese families give up their daughters for adoption. These laws are still in existence, though from time to time the government discusses whether or not to change them.

Home for New Year

The Chinese culture has traditionally emphasized relationships between people, especially people in one's family, as well as the relationship of the individual within society. Although the social network is very important,

A man burns incense to pay homage to his ancestors and to the gods of wealth, fortune, and health at Hong Kong's Che Kung Temple. Che Kung is a Chinese deity, and followers believe praying to Che Kung in the Lunar New Year will bring them good luck and wealth in the new year.

historically many Chinese people work far from home. Students have a similar problem—they often experience long periods of separation from their family and friends when they go to college. Like students in other countries, the Internet helps Chinese students feel less isolated.

Many university students eagerly look forward to New Year as an opportunity to reunite with families and friends, not just as a break from studies. The period around the first week of Chinese New Year is the time during which the greatest number of people in the world travel at one time (18 million in 2008) as students, Chinese migrant workers, and overseas Chinese around the world travel home for New Year's Eve. Everyone tries to get home in time for the elaborate dinner, which is usually held in or near the home of the oldest family member. In Taiwan, if someone cannot make it home, a place will be set at the table as though anticipating that member's arrival. This shows that the absent family member is present in thoughts of those at the celebration even if not physically there.

Those Chinese who, for whatever reason, cannot go home for the holiday often send bittersweet messages to those they love, sometimes as e-cards via the Internet or in the form of traditional Chinese New Year's cards. Such cards might show a serene landscape under a vast, empty sky and be accompanied by a verse from a poem or a phrase such as *"Tianya gong zhi shi."* ("Though we are at the farthest reaches of the world, yet we are close.") (Kozar 1994)

Different Days, Different Rituals

On Chinese New Year's Day itself, it is common for people to congratulate each other for having made it through another year. Everyone tries to be on his or her best behavior. People make an extra effort not to raise their voices, break anything, or tell lies that day. After the big reunion dinner the night before, families and friends play cards and board games, such as a Chinese variation of chess, *Xiangqi* (pronounced "Shiang-Chi"), sometimes known as "Elephant Chess." Other families prefer to watch gala New Year's programs on television.

The name for the third day of the Chinese New Year can be translated as "easy to get into arguments." Therefore, people try not to go visiting on the third day, for fear that conflict will arise. Also, families with relatives who died during the preceding three years usually visit their graves on the third day of the holiday. On the fifth day of the celebrations, many businesses reopen, especially because this day is the birthday of the god of wealth. Those who can do so take the whole 15-day New Year's period off, but not everyone can spend two weeks away from their duties.

Enter the Dragon

In city parks, whole families take part in open-air festivities during the 15 days of the New Year's holiday. Excited children laugh at the antics of jugglers and acrobats and the air is filled with the delicious fragrance of delicacies such as dumplings, dried fruits, and meats prepared by street vendors.

Lion dancers perform during the opening ceremony of the Temple of the Earth fair on the eve of Chinese New Year in Beijing. In addition to dragon dancing, lion dancing is often part of Chinese New Year celebrations.

Children feed red packets filled with "lucky money" to a lion in New York's Chinatown during celebrations commemorating the Lunar New Year. Children and unmarried adults are usually the recipients of the red packets, but these children chose to "feed" their packets to the lion, an animal representing bravery and peace, according to Chinese tradition.

Exploding firecrackers pop and crackle almost constantly, adding the sharp smell of flash powder to the air.

Mention Chinese New Year to someone in the United States and the image that probably comes to mind is of the dragon dance. In the dance, a team of people support a huge, brightly painted dragon's head, adorned with whiskers and spikes. Its gaping mouth and sharp teeth snap at the air. Sometimes the mouth is rigged to belch smoke. The dancers in front make the head dip and sway in imitation of the movement of a snake, as onlooking children step forward bravely, then giggle and run away from such a fierce beast.

All the people who carry the dragon must be agile and flexible, because they have to keep up with the other dancers while they coordinate the dragon's movements. It is hard work to create the convincing illusion of a magnificent creature that is also terrifying. The dancers who support the dragon's body make it twist and billow like the current of a river, because the dragon of the dragon dance is supposed to be a water spirit. People throw firecrackers at the dragons' feet during the parade, in order to "keep it awake" for the celebration. This is because according to Chinese legend, dragons sleep the rest of the year.

Five-, Four-, and Three-toed Dragons

Chinese dragons have five toes on each foot, Indonesian dragons have four, and Japanese dragons have three. The explanation given in Chinese legends is that the dragon loses its toes the farther it goes from its native China. By the time it reaches the end of Asia, it has lost all its toes and can go no farther. Its toes grow back if it returns to China. The Japanese offer a different explanation. They say that the dragon came from Japan and added toes the farther it traveled from Japan. By the time it got to China, it had so many toes it could no longer move.

Dragons are special to the Chinese, as well as to most Asians. They are supposed to bring good luck, prosperity, and fertility. Though their ferocious appearance can be frightening, they are considered wise and dignified supernatural beings. Whereas European dragons are generally seen as evil, Chinese dragons are viewed with respect. In China, nine is considered a lucky number. Chinese dragons are supposed to combine the physical traits of nine animals, including the scales of a fish, the body of a serpent, and the claws of a tiger. These traits enable them to be at home in the air,

A boy gives a red packet to a lion dancer, performing at a temple during the first day of Chinese New Year celebration in Kuala Lumpur, Malaysia.

on the land, and in the water. Not surprisingly, the dragon dance is often the highlight of Chinese New Year, and in most Asian countries there are many legends, myths, and stories involving dragons.

Bang! Pop! Kaboom!

It used to be that no Chinese New Year's celebration would be complete without fireworks. After a late night feast, everyone used to gather in the street in anticipation. At midnight, the crowd would cheer as they heard the first "thunk" of the rockets being launched, followed by the sight of trails of sparks climbing up through the sky. Suddenly, the dark sky above would blossom into luminous showers of color accompanied by white flashes of light. A moment later, the earsplitting booms of the firecrackers would reach the spectators' ears.

While this scene is still part of Chinese New Year's in many countries, the fireworks displays have been turned over to the local governments because of the number of injuries and fires caused by fireworks in the past. Pollution from the smoke and debris has also been a factor in regulating fireworks. In places such as Hong Kong, civic leaders now entertain 400,000 excited spectators with a yearly fireworks presentation over Victoria Harbor on the second day of New Year.

Lanterns and Sticky Rice Cakes

Before the 15th day of the New Year, shopkeepers put up huge lanterns. There are lanterns of every imaginable color, size, and shape. The display

The Origin of Fireworks

Fireworks are believed to have originated in China more than 2,000 years ago as a result of using gunpowder for military purposes. The Chinese named it *huo yao*, or "fire chemical." Firecrackers were probably invented by a monk named Li Tuan about 1,000 years ago. The loud bangs supposedly frighten off ghosts and evil spirits. Recently, many countries that hold Chinese New Year's celebrations have been forced to outlaw firecrackers because of the number of injuries that have resulted from their use, as well as the pollution they can cause when exploded in great numbers.

A customer selects a Chinese lantern at a shop in Malaysia, for the Lunar New Year, celebrated by ethnic Chinese around the world.

reaches its most dazzling when Yuan Xyiao, the Lantern Festival, takes place after dark on the 15th day of the Chinese New Year. This day marks the first full Moon of the year, and once again families gather together to celebrate. They eat a sticky rice cake to symbolize unity, or "sticking together as a family." There are two main kinds of rice cakes: *yuan xiao* and *yang tuan*. From the outside they look the same—much like white, slightly lumpy Ping-Pong balls. They are stuffed with one of two kinds of fillings: sweet ingredients or salty, non-sweet mixtures. The usual sweet fillings combine some mix of sugar, red bean paste, sesame seeds, walnut, sweetened tangerine peel, and peanuts. Some cooks use only one ingredient for each filling, but others combine ingredients. The most common non-sweet filling is ground pork, but minced vegetables or a mixture of meat and vegetables is also popular.

The rice flour that is used for covering the filling is what is known as glutinous or sticky rice. The stickiness of the dough holds the pastry together. The difference between *yuan xiao* and *yang tuan* lies in how they are formed and the type of filling inserted in each, which varies between northern and southern China. In northern China, *yang tuan*, with the sweet and non-meat fillings, are more common. *Yang tuan* are made by

Taiwanese launch balloon lanterns inscribed with hopes and wishes for the new year as part of the Lantern Festival.

forming the dough into a ball, making a hole, and inserting the filling. Assembling the non-sweet *yuan xiao*, popular in southern China, is a bit more complicated. The filling is shaped first, dipped lightly in water, then rolled in a basket containing the dry rice flour. The water causes a layer of flour to stick to the filling. Then the coated filling is dipped into water a second time, and rolled in more flour. Layers are added one by one, just like rolling a ball of snow to make a snowman. When the dumpling is the desired size, it is dumped in boiling water to cook.

The Lantern Festival signals the end of the Chinese New Year's holidays. Everyone returns to his or her usual routine. Business resumes and students return to school.

Conclusion

Both the Chinese and the Western calendar-based December 31/January 1 New Year's celebrations place great emphasis on the need to redeem past errors and prepare the way for the future. Chinese New Year maintains a tie to the original agricultural origins of the New Year while incorpo-

Fireworks explode over Hong Kong's Victoria Harbor as the former British colony celebrates Chinese New Year.

rating more modern forms of celebration. Its practices have been refined over time, resulting in a cohesive, singular holiday. The traditions of the Western New Year are more about marking time in the general sense. Customs vary from place to place, finding common ground in the symbolic excitement of a new beginning. Taken together, the two holidays solidify New Year as the most universal celebration of all. No one can escape the passage of time, but for people worldwide the rituals of the Chinese and Western New Year help give it shape and substance.

A man in a traditional Chinese outfit wishes spectators a happy New Year during the Chinese New Year Parade in Vancouver, Canada. Thousands of people line the streets of Chinatown to watch the annual parade.

Regional Traditions and Customs

⊚ ⊚ ⊚

Africa

In many parts of Africa, the New Year's holiday is not much more than a legal holiday, a day without school or work. People may celebrate it, but there are no elaborate festivities. This is true in the northern country of Algeria, as well as the western African countries of Burkina Faso and Ghana and in the islands of São Tomé and Principe. In the southern countries of Namibia, Swaziland, and Angola, the holiday is also quiet. For the people of Eritrea, South Africa, and Tanzania, however, New Year is a robust celebration.

New Year Is a Day of Remembrance in Eritrea

In eastern Africa lies the country of Eritrea. The population is a mixture of Muslims and Christians. January 1 is important in Eritrea for several reasons. Not only is this New Year's Day, but it is also a day of remembrance. It is a time when the people honor those who struggled in the country's fight for independence from Ethiopia. In 1952, the United Nations recommended that Eritrea join with Ethiopia in what is known as a federation. (A federation is when two semi-self-governing countries are joined under a central, or federal, government.) However, the ruler of Ethiopia, Emperor Haile Selassie I (1892–1975), ignored the UN resolution and made Eritrea Ethiopia's 14th province. His decision set off a civil war that lasted 30 years.

The Eritreans were finally able to become independent of Ethiopia on May 24, 1993, and beginning in 1994 January 1 has

In the Cape Province of South Africa, New Year's celebrations take on a carnival atmosphere. Here, a boy with his face painted blows a whistle in celebration.

The Eritrean National Anthem

The Eritrean National Anthem commemorates Eritrea's struggle for independence from Ethiopia. It is frequently sung on New Year's Day, which doubles as an independence day for that country. Here is an English translation of the anthem:

Eritrea, Eritrea, Eritrea,
Her enemy decimated
and her sacrifices vindicated by liberation.
Steadfast in her goal,
symbolizing endurance,
Eritrea, the pride of her oppressed people,
proved that the truth prevails.

CHORUS
Eritrea, Eritrea
holds her rightful place in the world.
Dedication that led to liberation
Will build up and make her green
We shall honor her with progress
We have a word for her to embellish

become nationally important as a day dedicated to looking ahead and renewing efforts to make the country prosperous and self-sufficient.

A Carnival Atmosphere in South Africa

The country of South Africa is located at the southernmost tip of Africa. The country shares borders to the north with Swaziland, Mozambique, Zimbabwe, Botswana, and Namibia. The residents of South Africa celebrate December 31 and January 1 as the New Year's holiday, and New Year's Eve parties last all night. New Year's Day is greeted with the sounds of church bells and fireworks displays. In South Africa's Cape Province, the atmosphere is like a carnival. People wear brightly colored clothes, paint their faces, and dance for hours.

Climbing Mount Kilimanjaro to Celebrate the New Year

Many visitors to Tanzania celebrate the beginning of the New Year by climbing Mount Kilimanjaro. Despite Mount Kilimanjaro's height (19,340 feet), it is known as "Everyman's Everest." (Mount Everest, at 29,028 feet, is the tallest mountain in the world. It is located in the Himalayan mountains in Asia.) There are a number of routes—ranging from easy to difficult—up to the top of Kilimanjaro. This makes it attractive to climbers of all skill levels. The whole trip up and back usually takes about five days.

Celebrating New Year's in Tanzania

Tanzania is the largest country in eastern Africa. It has two large mountains in the northeast, Mount Meru and Mount Kilimanjaro. The highest mountain in Africa, Kilimanjaro measures 19,340 feet.

In Tanzania, New Year's Eve and New Year's Day are cause for parties and celebrating. Dodoma, the capital city, is filled with people waving the national flag and riding in cars decorated with the national colors: green, black, blue, and yellow. There is cheering, honking, and a general party atmosphere throughout the night.

Many tourists travel to Tanzania around this time to greet the new year from the summit of Mount Kilimanjaro.

Asia

Most countries in Asia celebrate December 31 and January 1 as public, legal holidays. However, because of religious and cultural differences, the attitude toward beginning the new year on January 1 varies greatly. In countries with large Chinese populations January 1 is a legal holiday. Chinese New Year, however, is when they hold their "real" New Year's celebrations. For countries such as India, where Hinduism is the principal religion, Diwali is the festive New Year celebration (and January 1 is not particularly important). Countries with large Muslim populations such as Indonesia follow the Islamic calendar, so their New Year takes place at an entirely different time.

The New Year Begins January 14 in Azerbaijan

Once part of the Soviet Union, the country of Azerbaijan was officially created after the breakup of the USSR in 1991. Although the Soviets tried to suppress Islam, the majority of people in Azerbaijan are Muslims. The remainder of the country is mainly Orthodox Christian. Despite high unemployment and a low standard of living, the country has a rich culture and literary heritage, especially in the field of poetry. Quite liberal for a Muslim-majority country, Azerbaijan enjoys a blend of both Islamic and European cultures. As in many other parts of the world, family and friends toast each other with sweet chocolate or cherry liqueurs at midnight on New Year's Eve, wishing each other a happy New Year. The people of Azerbaijan have a strong tradition of hospitality. According to one of their proverbs, "A guest is a light in the house." It is considered good luck to have guests on New Year's Day as a way of renewing the spirit of friendship within the home.

On New Year's Eve, Azerbaijanis also decorate a tree (not unlike a Christmas tree). These trees stay up and decorated until at least January 13. To the Azerbaijani, this is the official end of the old year. Children then receive gifts on January 1. The children believe these gifts are delivered on December 31 from Shakta Babah (the Azerbaijani name for the Russian Ded Moroz, Grandfather Frost) and Snegurochka (his granddaughter).

A dragon head is carried high by a Hong Kong dragon dance troupe as spectators watch the opening ceremony of the annual Chinese New Year Parade in Hong Kong.

The Family's Report Card in China

In Chinese homes, it is a common custom to offer biannual sacrifices to Zao Jun, the kitchen god. Chinese families place a paper representation of Zao Jun inside on New Year's Day. They believe both Zao Jun and his wife reside there, and that his wife records what the family says and does during the upcoming year.

Offerings and incense are burned for the kitchen god twice a year—once on his birthday (the third day of the eighth lunar month) and once on the 23rd day of the 12th lunar month, just before the Chinese New Year. After the second instance, it is believed that he is summoned to heaven by the Jade Emperor, the supreme ruler of heaven, to report on the family's behavior over the past year. Thus families often make sugarcane offerings to Zao Jun or else smear his lips with honey in hopes that it will

Birthdays and the New Year in China

Chinese tradition says that all people were born on the seventh day of the new year. Therefore, people in China add another year to their age—and celebrate their birthdays—on that day rather than on the anniversary of their birth.

sweeten his report—or keep his lips stuck together! Firecrackers are also customarily lit to hurry the kitchen god on his way to heaven. After all of this, the paper figure is burned and replaced with a new one on New Year's Day.

Celebrating January 1 and Hindu New Year in India

India is a vast country encompassing more than 1 million square miles. India's neighbors are Pakistan, Nepal, Myanmar, Bhutan, China, Bangladesh, and Sri Lanka. It is bordered by the Arabian Sea, the Indian Ocean, and the Bay of Bengal. Most Indians are Hindu. In 1498 Portuguese explorer Vasco da Gama sailed to India. The Portuguese controlled India for about the next 450 years. Over the years, the French, Dutch, and the United Kingdom have tried to rule India. Both the British and the French established trading posts in India in the 17th century. This rivalry escalated to war in the 18th century resulting in British victory. India gained its independence from Great Britain in 1947.

In India the time for the New Year is set by the Hindu lunar calendar. Nevertheless, the people also celebrate December 31 and January 1, just as most people who live by the Gregorian calendar do. The people of India enjoy having parties, watching fireworks, and making resolutions, or goals, for the coming year. Many of these parties have dress codes that require bright colors or unique fabrics to heighten the festive atmosphere. There may be bonfires or outdoor concerts. Actors and actresses from the hugely popular Indian film industry make public appearances, singing songs and dancing with the revelers.

Bamboo, Plum, and Pine Branch Decorations in Japan

Japan is comprised of islands. Although there are four main islands, the country encompasses more than 3,000 islands, stretching from north to south for approximately 2,000 miles.

The Japanese have been influenced by both Western and traditional Asian culture, and these influences are reflected in their celebrations. Though it originally followed the lunar calendar, in 1873 Japan adopted the Gregorian calendar, so New Year's festivities now run from January 1 to 3. Shogatsu and Oshogatsu (both literally meaning "new month"),

Bamboo Filled with Water and Sand in Case of Fire

The *kadomatsu* arrangement may have originated from the Edo period in Japan (1603–1867), when giant pieces of bamboo were filled with water and sand, and placed at doorways in case of fire.

are Japanese names for New Year. Shops and schools are closed for these three days. People send special New Year's postcards (*nengajo*) to each other, similar to the practice of sending Christmas cards. These are often decorated with the animal that corresponds to the Chinese zodiac.

The Japanese use branches of bamboo, plum, and pine trees tied with straw to decorate their homes in an elaborate arrangement known as a *kadomatsu*. *Kadomatsu* are part of the Shinto tradition. Shintoism is the principal religion or philosophy of Japan. Like Daoism and Buddhism (also practiced by many Japanese), Shintoism is more of an approach toward life than a religion in the Western sense. In Shintoism, everything has a spirit or soul, known as *kami*. The purpose of the *kadomatsu* is to welcome good *kami* and to invite prayer. Often one *kadomatsu* is placed on each side of the doorway, like soldiers standing guard. At entrances to public buildings and shopping centers the *kadomatsu* are much larger than those for the home—often 7 or 8 feet tall.

The symbolism behind these arrangements is appropriate for New Year: Bamboo stands for growth and strength, the pine for long life, and the plum for constancy, since it brings sweet flowers after enduring the cold Japanese winters. There are specific rules about how the arrangement should be put together, too. For example, the bamboo should be sliced at various heights, angled to "allow the spirits to enter," it must come in contact with the floor. Placing it in a bucket or container is considered bad luck.

Other preparations for the new year are similar to those of Chinese New Year. People thoroughly clean their homes, pay off their debts, and cook mountains of food so that they can enjoy the holidays in a relaxed

(opposite page) A huge red lantern written with Chinese characters meaning "Gate of the Wind and Thunder God" is hung over New Year's worshippers at the Asakusa Sensoji Temple in downtown Tokyo, Japan. A half million people visit the famed temple each day during the New Year's holiday to pray for a good year and health.

way, greeting the new year with a fresh start. Most of the food is prepared in advance.

Homes are decorated to honor the *kami* of the house. In addition to placing *kadomatsu* in front of homes, it is also customary to place a *shimenawa* at the entrance to the house or over the stove. A *shimenawa* is a rope made from freshly braided rice straw. The Shinto belief is that no evil can get past the sacred boundary of the *shimenawa*. Colors at this time are chosen for their symbolic meanings, too. Red symbolizes the Sun and its powerful energy, whereas white stands for purity and innocence.

In December, people attend *bonenkai* (year-forgetting) parties. These are not the family gatherings that take place between January 1 and 3. Instead, these are usually parties attended by employees, their bosses, and business friends, or gatherings of students from the same college or university. The favorite place to hold *bonenkais* is at restaurants that serve drinks. (*Shinnekai*, or parties celebrating the New Year, will be held in January.)

Because the Japanese have converted to the Gregorian calendar and shortened their New Year's festivities from 15 days to three days, the day

Japanese worshippers fill the area around Tokyo's Zojoji Temple as balloons with New Year's resolutions are released at midnight on January 1.

Buddhist priests toll the huge bronze bell at a temple in Kyoto, Japan. The bell, which weighs 70 tons, is one of the three largest temple bells in Japan. Traditionally, at Buddhist temples, devotees strike the bell 108 times to cleanse themselves of 108 worldly desires and start a fresh new year.

before New Year's Day is now devoted to games and fun, especially kite flying. January 1 and 2 are feast days with family and times for visiting the local temple.

On New Year's Eve, the end-of-the-year bell (*joya no kane*) is struck in all Buddhist temples 108 times. Each toll of the bell is timed to come only after the sound of the previous vibration has died away. In Buddhist tradition, the sound of the bell represents the leaving behind of the previous year's worries and concerns. The last peal of the bell takes place at midnight, ushering in a new year with new opportunities.

An Herbal Health Drink for the New Year

The Japanese drink *otoso* originated in China and originally contained eight herbs. Some of the herbs have been substituted for others over the years, probably because some people decided the original herbs were too strong. Still, the *otoso* of today contains much the same ingredients as the beverage the Japanese adopted from the Chinese in the ninth century. At that time, the herbs would be placed in a triangular bag and hung from the branch of a peach tree that reached out over water. At 4 A.M. the herbs were placed in the sake and allowed to sit for several hours until the *otoso* was needed for toasting the new year. The original belief was that if one family member drank *otoso* on New Year's morning, the family would stay healthy all year long. If all the family members drank it, the whole village would enjoy good health for the year.

People like to wake up early on New Year's Day in order to see the sunrise, which is thought to bring good fortune and luck in the new year. They often put on new clothes, then head off to visit family shrines to make offerings of money or other donations. Having observed these rituals, they sit down to enjoy the hearty soup known as *ozoni,* which has

A Busy Time for Postal Workers

Since the Japan Post Service promises to deliver all the postcards that are mailed by a certain date in time for New Year's Day, students work as part-time postal carriers to ensure that everyone gets their cards on time. After a 10-year privatization of the country's postal services began in 2007, new providers held New Year's ceremonies to mark their dedication to delivering as many cards as possible on New Year's Day.

Fireworks explode over residents paying a traditional New Year's visit to a shrine in northern Japan at midnight on January 1.

many variations but is always made with the sticky rice cakes called *mochi*. Families then toast the New Year with *otoso*, sweet sake (rice wine) that has been flavored with cinnamon, rhubarb (a leafy green vegetable), Japanese pepper, and other herbs. *Otoso* is reputed to prevent sickness and encourage peace in the household. The sake must be drunk in special cups and poured from a special vessel that looks much like a teapot. Those who follow the custom in the traditional way have the youngest member of the household drink first and the oldest drink last. The idea is that each person gets to share in the joys of youth.

The foods served during New Year's are specifically chosen for their symbolism, just as they are in other countries. Fish eggs, in this case herring and salmon eggs, are customarily served for the holidays because they represent fertility. One type of dinner enjoyed during New Year by the Japanese is known as *shabu-shabu*, a dish consisting of thinly sliced beef or fish and vegetables cooked briefly in simmering broth. Before it's made, the sliced beef, fish, and vegetables are set on trays. Each person chooses which foods to eat, then cooks them in a communal pan in the middle of the table. A similar process takes place in a self-serve sushi dinner. Each diner receives seaweed wrappers, a bowl of sushi rice, and small bowls filled with wasabi (Japanese horseradish) and dipping sauce. Family members then put together their own sushi from an extensive selection of foods and fillings.

Divided Celebrations in a Divided Korea

The countries of North Korea and South Korea also celebrate the New Year's Eve and New Year's Day holidays. However, because North Korea remains under communist rule, and South Korea is a democracy, their celebrations are different. Under the communist dictatorship public religious practices have disappeared. Still, businesses are closed for January 1 in North Korea so that families can celebrate the public holiday. For both countries Seollal, the Lunar New Year, occasions a three-day public holiday about a month after Gregorian New Year.

Owing to the political and other freedoms and liberties of its citizenry, South Korea celebrates the New Year with far more spirit than North Korea. The first and second of January are both South Korean holidays. In Seoul, South Korea's capital city, people sing, dance, and party through the night of December 31 and there are fireworks at midnight.

Because South Korea enjoys mild weather at the beginning of January, it is popular to go to the beach and watch the sunrise on the first day of the new year. (New Year's Day is called Sinjeong.) It is believed that if a person makes a wish at sunrise, the wish will come true. Many seaside towns hold "sunrise festivals," some of them large-scale. Events such as fireworks, musical concerts, candle lighting, and ringing in the new year are all common. The most commonly served food is rice-cake soup (*tteok-guk*). There are many variations on the soup, some calling for anchovy broth, others for beef, or both (*guk* means broth). Some versions include sliced cooked eggs, marinated meat, dumplings (*mandu*), and dried seaweed for seasoning. What all the recipes have in common is the rice cake. This soup, which is supposed to bring good luck and health in the coming year, is also eaten later in the year to celebrate the Lunar New Year. But it is tricky to eat. Apparently it is so slippery it almost slides down the throat, but gooey enough that it really needs to be chewed.

Fireworks explode over a crowd of people gathering to celebrate New Year in Seoul, South Korea, on January 1.

South Korean men wearing traditional dress bow to their village head man in observance of Seollal, the Lunar New Year, in a small village in South Korea. In a country of about 49 million people, as many as 34 million return to their hometowns for family reunions and traditional ancestral rights during the three-day Lunar New Year holiday.

In South Korea, Gyeongpo Beach in the town of Jeongdongjin is a favorite spot for watching the sunrise all year round, so it is especially popular during New Year's celebrations. The town has some rather strange claims to fame. For example, the train station in Jeongdongjin is closer to the beach than any station anywhere else in the world. There is also a sculpture park surrounded by two real cruise ships. The ships sit on the cliffs overlooking the harbor, as if they sailed in and got stuck when they tried to sail away. Today the cruise ships house restaurants and condominiums.

Burn the Bad and Let the Good Soar

At some sunrise festivals in South Korea, participants write their misfortunes from the previous year on a piece of paper, then burn them, symbolizing the end of those misfortunes. Other festivals take a different approach: Participants write their wishes for the new year, place them in helium-filled balloons, and then release them.

A South Korean dancer wearing a traditional lion mask performs during the Kangnyoung Mask Dance, a popular performance to celebrate the Lunar New Year holiday in Seoul, South Korea.

Jeongdongjin's Hourglass Park, also at the beach, is named after what was once the largest hourglass in the world. This hourglass is not shaped like the ones in Western pictures of Father Time, with one glass bulb above another connected by a narrow tube. It looks more like a gigantic drum lying on its side. At midnight on the last day of the year the hourglass is turned and the sand inside begins to fall. It takes 13 minutes to turn the gigantic structure and an entire year for the sand inside to drain into the lower part of the drum. Gyeongpo Beach also contributes to the sunrise festival with fireworks and music concerts, and other events such as swimming competitions, or running on the white sand beach.

A few weeks after the celebration of the solar New Year's, both North and South Koreans observe a three-day public holiday for Seollal, lunar new year's day. On Seotdal Geumeum, New Year's Eve, people eat mixed rice with vegetables (*bibimbap*), bean powder rice cakes (*injeolmi*), and traditional biscuits (*hangwa*). By tradition Koreans stay up all night and leave their doors open on Seotdal Geumeum so ancestral spirits can come in. To ward off evil spirits, straw shovels or rakes are placed at the doors of houses on this night. On Seollal itself, Koreans adorn themselves in their traditional dress—*hanbok*—and perform *charye*, the practice of waking early and setting a table to honor the past four generations of ancestors.

Ceremonial food is prepared and placed on the *charye sang*, or ceremonial table, in a particular order. Then, incense sticks are lit and family members take turns bowing before their ancestors. The eldest member of the family bows twice in front of the ancestors, and then, after making a shallow bow, offers drink and food to the ancestral spirits. The rest of the family follows suit in order of seniority. Then the living members turn away from the offerings to allow the ancestral spirits to enjoy their food. After some time, the table is cleared.

The living members of the family show their respect toward their elders by performing *sebae* (a formal bow of respect) before all the elders of the family and wishing them *bok*, or good fortune, in the coming year. In return the elders give money, gifts, and advice to the younger generation.

A traditional meal of *ttok-guk* (rice cake soup with thick beef broth) is served to the family members. South Koreans believe that in order to grow a year older one must consume *ttok-guk* on Seollal. Other popular foods eaten on Seollal are *chapchae* (noodles with meat and vegetables), *yakshik* (sticky sweet rice), *pindaettok* (bean pancakes), *shike* (rice punch), and *sujonggwa* (cinnamon-flavored persimmon punch).

A Cold New Year in Mongolia

The country of Mongolia is located in northern Asia, situated between Russia and China. Nearly all of its 3 million people are Mongal, and half of them are Buddhists. Very few holidays are observed in Mongolia because of the years of communist repression it experienced. January 1 is one of the few holidays that is celebrated. It is probably because of Mongolia's long history of Russian influence that Mongolians maintain this tradition of the Western New Year as well as their own lunar-based new year, Tsagaan Tsar. Technically, Tsagaan Tsar occurs around the time Chinese New Year does, but the Mongolians generally deny Chinese influence so do not recognize it as such.

On the Gregorian New Year, Ulaanbaatar, the capital of Mongolia, is the coldest capital in the world. As a result, on December 31 it is not uncommon to find several thousand Mongolian cele-

Mongolians pray at a Buddhist monastery in Ulaanbaatar, Mongolia. Mongolia has been rediscovering its Buddhist heritage since the end of one-party rule in 1990. Nearly half the people of Mongolia are Buddhist and embrace the Lunar New Year.

Star Wars Costumes Were Based on Traditional Mongolian Dress

The costume designers of *Star Wars Episode I: The Phantom Menace* were so intrigued by Mongolian dress they used the traditional clothing of a Mongolian noblewoman as the inspiration behind Queen Amidala's senate costume, which features rich embroidered fabrics, an elaborate headdress, and an upright collar that rises behind her head like the hood of a cobra. Mongolian influences show up in the film's other costumes as well.

brants waiting for midnight outside at a temperature of minus-30 degrees Fahrenheit or colder. The Mongolian clothing for this kind of event includes plenty of layers, some of them fur. Typically, the women wear bright colors and heavy jewelry, making an exotic contrast to their huge sheepskin coats and snow leopardskin sashes.

Just before midnight, fireworks begin to blaze across the sky. Bonfires are lit and entertainers dressed like the famous Mongol ruler Genghis Khan (ca. 1162–1227) interact with the crowds. (Genghis Khan founded and ruled the Mongol Empire by uniting nomadic tribes.) At midnight itself, the noise rises to a crescendo, as exploding fireworks, cheering crowds, flying bottle rockets, and even train whistles signal the beginning of a new year.

Weeks later Mongolians celebrate the Lunar New Year of Tsagaan Tsar, which means "white month (or moon)" in English. The lunar new year celebration depends on the cycles of the Moon and can fall anytime between the end of January and early March. The color white stands for purity, happiness, wealth, and well-being. Tsagaan Tsar is the start of the lactating and breeding period of cattle. and the people anticipate that spring will bring an abundance of dairy products. Families start planning for the holidays a month in advance, preparing plenty of food and gifts. Houses, *gers* (tents), and sheds are all given a thorough cleaning before the new year. On Tsagaan Tsar, as on other Mongolian holidays, people sing songs and play games. The New Year's Eve corresponding to Tsagaan Tsar is called Bituun—the last dinner of the old year. The following morning, everyone awakes early to greet the rising Sun, then family members exchange greetings and gifts.

The value of the gift is not important; often it is merely some socks, a pack of cigarettes, or a bottle of drink. Mongolians celebrate the New Year for three days full of eating and drinking fermented mare's milk, *airag*, and *arkhi*, vodka. In the past people went to an *ovoo*, an arrangement of stones on a hilltop, with trays of food and other offerings to show their gratitude to nature. During the 16 days of the New Year celebrations, a number of rites devoted to the 12 miracles of Buddha are performed, and fire plays a very important part. One of these rituals, called Sor, is observed during the lunar New Year celebrations. When the fire, *sora*, gains strength, its sparks fly high into the cold winter sky, and the participants toss lumps of red dough, which symbolize enemies of the faith, into the blazing fire. This ritual is one of the final episodes of the holiday of the White Moon. In another New Year ritual, people burn their misfortunes in the fire and make wishes for the coming year: May the fire in the hearth burn (may it be warm at home) and may everybody enjoy good health.

Money for Good Luck in the Philippines

The population of the Philippine islands is close to 90 million, about one quarter the size of the population in the United States. The islands form an archipelago, or group of islands, in Southeast Asia, east of the country of Vietnam. The major ethnic groups are Malay (95 percent) and Chinese. In contrast to the Mongols, the people of the Philippines are mostly Christian. More than 80 percent of the country is Roman Catholic, with another 9 percent Protestant. Most Filipinos attend mass at midnight on New Year's Eve and pray that the new year will be a good one. After the church ceremonies, they have a late dinner called Media Noche. At this meal, among other things, they serve a dozen types of round fruit, each one representing a different month of the year. Eating round foods and wearing clothes with polka dots or circular designs is considered good luck because the circle symbolizes completion, wholeness, and the round shape of coins. New Year's is also the time for Filipinos to wear their new clothes, usually in colors of red and gold.

Another Filipino custom is to fill one's pockets with money. At midnight, people shake their clothes, making the coins jingle. This is another way to bring good luck. The idea is that money will flow to the place where money already exists. In addition, on the eve of the new year, Filipinos like to open their doors and windows, leave the lights on, and place coins on their doorsteps. These customs are performed to invite good luck and good fortune into their homes.

Filipino fruit vendors sell a lot of fruit during the holiday rush at a market in Manila, Philippines. Many Filipinos buy round-shaped fruits believing that it will bring them good luck in the coming new year.

Chinese Filipinos have additional traditions for December 31 and January 1. They light firecrackers on New Year's Eve to scare off any bad spirits. Families get together at midnight to beat on drums, pans, or anything else that will make a loud noise.

A Big Chinese New Year in Taiwan

Chinese New Year, also known as the Lunar New Year and the Spring Festival, are celebrated in Taiwan with great joy. Around mid-December, weeks before the celebrations begin on New Year's Eve, people in Taiwan start their preparations. There is great excitement because New Year's is a time when entire families gather for dinner, if possible. If someone is unable to make the trip home for the celebration, a place setting is still placed on the table; it symbolizes the person's presence in spirit, if not in body. After dinner youngsters are given cash gifts by their elders and everyone stays up late to see the old year out and to welcome in the new one.

The Chinese New Year is a two-week holiday filled with festivities as well as piety. The Taiwanese begin the next day with prayer and worship. This day is set aside to meet and greet friends and relatives and the streets are filled with throngs of people on their way to reunions or watching dragon dancing, lion dancing, and other traditional forms of entertainment and activities that take place on the streets. Families get together to share special feasts on this day. Streets and homes are decorated with colorful lanterns and elaborate lighting and there are firework displays all over Taiwan.

On the second day of the new year, married women return home to visit their families. (The third day is regarded as a bad day for visiting relatives.) On the fourth day a host of deities who made a trip to heaven to report the activities of individual families return to take up their vigil once more, and most people go back to work after celebrating for four or five days. On the 13th and 14th days shopkeepers are open again, and they hang lanterns out for the Lantern Festival (Yuen Siu). The festivities continue until the colorful Lantern Festival, on the 15th day of the new year, before life again returns to its routine.

Two shoppers sample sweets as they shop in Taipei, Taiwan, for New Year's supplies ranging from candy, nuts, fruits, and vegetables to dried fish, Chinese herbs and teas, and even decorations.

Though the traditional festivities associated with the Chinese New Year are millennia old, they still have great importance. Cleaning and rearranging one's home improves cleanliness and symbolizes a fresh start; worshiping ancestors and deities upholds filial piety and family ethics; sitting around the hearth together symbolizes unity and the value of spending important occasions with one's family; and making New Year's visits home after marriage maintains

Vietnam's Most Important Holiday

Also located in Southeast Asia, the country of Vietnam celebrates the first day of the first month of the Chinese lunar calendar. This day is called Tet Nguyen Dan, or Tet, and its name means "the festival of the first day." Tet is the most important holiday in Vietnam. Like the Chinese, the Vietnamese have a kitchen god known as "Ong Dao." Although his basic role is the same as in China (to report on the family's behavior during the year about to end), aspects

Vietnamese women light incense and pray at a pagoda in Ho Chi Minh City, Vietnam, in observance of Vietnam's biggest holiday, Tet, the Lunar New Year.

of his personality and the customs surrounding him are slightly different. In Vietnam, there are actually three kitchen gods represented by the three legs that support the cooking equipment. They are known as "Dao Quan." Two of them are believed to be male and the other female.

Tet is based on the same calendar used by the Chinese, but Tet and Chinese New Year do not always coincide, simply because of the time difference between Beijing and Hanoi, the capital of Vietnam. Both holidays, however, share such customs as dragon dances and firework displays to scare away evil spirits. In Vietnam, the celebrations last for a week. New Year is considered the holiest time of the year. Some dishes are made and eaten only during Tet, such as dried candied fruits (*mut*); a banana-leaf wrap of rice, pork, and bean puree (*banh chung*); and roasted watermelon seeds (*hat dua*).

Europe

In Europe, several countries celebrate December 31 not only as New Year's Eve but as Saint Sylvester's feast day. Sylvester is associated with a number of legends, including the one in which he bound the mouth of a dragon and then brought its victims back to life.

Other customs common throughout Europe are fireworks displays, which become particularly noisy at midnight, and eating and drinking wonderful arrays of special foods and sparkling wines. Parades are common in the large cities such as Rome, and thousands gather at Saint Peter's square to receive the pope's blessings. Often shows and concerts are specially organized for New Year's Eve, lasting long into the night.

Elegant Parties in Austria

For Austrians, New Year's Eve is called Sylvesterabend, or Saint Sylvester's Eve. Balls and other elaborate parties are held in Vienna, Austria's capital, as well as in other cities. The Vienna State Opera and the Vienna Philharmonic give concerts on both days, which are televised to many listeners around the world.

The traditional New Year's concert given by the Vienna Philharmonic orchestra at the "Golden Hall" of the Musikverein in Vienna, Austria.

Lucky Pork and Lentils in the Czech Republic

People in the Czech Republic enjoy a special meal with lentils and pork on New Year's Day. Pork is believed to bring good luck and the lentils good health and prosperity. Whereas the Chinese consider fish a lucky symbol for the new year, New Year's meals in the Czech Republic deliberately exclude any fish or poultry. Czech tradition has it that fish can make one's good luck swim away, and poultry can make one's luck fly away.

Broken Dishes in Denmark

North of Germany is the country of Denmark. Denmark is made up of more than 400 islands, but people live on only about 82 of them. On New Year's Eve, people throughout the kingdom of Denmark watch their country's king make a televised speech. On New Year's Day it is a positive thing to find many broken dishes on one's doorstep, since it is considered good luck. Friends traditionally place the pieces there. People will save their broken dishes throughout the year specifically for this purpose.

Kissing under the Mistletoe in France

In France, people usually eat traditional foods to usher in the new year. One of these is *soupe à l'oignon*, or onion soup, which is covered with cheese and contains chunks of bread. Another is *dinde rôtie*, or roast turkey. Still

A Mock Protest in France

At the end of 2006, hundreds of French protesters in the western city of Nantes held a mocking protest against the year 2007. They carried banners reading "No to 2007!" and "Now is better!" They also called on governments and the United Nations to stop Time's "mad race" by declaring a moratorium or temporary suspension of the future. When rain fell on the protesters, they joked that even the weather was against the new year. As the last minutes of 2006 ticked away, they began to chant "No to 2007!" When the year arrived despite their opposition, they vowed to make the protest an annual event.

The new year is welcomed with fireworks in Cologne, Germany. Thousands of people meet in the Old Town to watch the fireworks.

others will have pancakes because they are thought to bring good luck. The first day of the new year is the time to visit friends, neighbors, and relatives and to exchange gifts. Whereas in the United States it is traditional to hang mistletoe and kiss under it during the Christmas season, in France it is customary to do so just as the new year begins.

Leave Food on Your Plate in Germany

In Germany New Year's Eve and New Year's Day are for long-lasting parties and fireworks. To some, New Year's Eve is called Sylvester, named after a German pope from the fourth century. This is because December 31 is the feast of Saint Sylvester.

It is a German New Year's Eve custom not to eat everything on one's dinner plate and not to clear the table until midnight. This is done to make sure there is plenty of food and drink to be had in the new year. Fortune-telling is also an old German New Year's tradition. There are a variety of games played at this time to predict what the new year will bring.

Snake-Shaped Cake in Italy

Italy is a peninsula in southern Europe. Shaped like a boot, the country is surrounded by water on three sides. Italians celebrate New Year's Eve by giving children gifts and money. People attend church the next morning, and enjoy the day with friends and family. As part of lunch, a snake-shaped cake is often served. The cake symbolizes new beginnings, since a snake sheds its old skin after a new skin has grown.

In Vatican City, which has its own government within the city of Rome representing Roman Catholic Church, New Year's Day is celebrated as the World Day of Peace. The pope, head of the Roman Catholic Church, says a special mass for peace on this day. His words are transmitted directly to heads of state around the world and also through broadcasts on television and radio to Catholics in many countries.

Fortune-Telling in Lithuania

Lithuania lies between Russia and Latvia. It shares borders with both Belarus and Poland. In 1990, Lithuania declared its independence from the Soviet Union, although this was not recognized until 1991. As in Germany, fortune-telling is important to New Year's celebrations in the Republic of Lithuania. People want to know about their chances for love, marriage, career growth or change, and health in the months to come. Fortune-telling is so common that people even ask for predictions about the weather. If it snows on New Year's Eve, tradition holds there will be a snowy winter. If the weather is good, then the country will enjoy a good harvest in the coming year.

Sleigh Rides in Poland

Poland lies in central Europe to the east of Germany. Here it has long been a tradition to go on sleigh rides on New Year's Day. Long ago, people would use the sleighs to go from town to town, dancing together and celebrating the holiday. Today some keep the tradition just for fun. Many Poles attend fancy parties, or balls. Poles also recognize Saint Sylvester's feast day on December 31. They often

A Polish woman gets into her car with a bunch of balloons on New Year's Eve. Balloons are a popular decoration at New Year's parties in Poland.

Two girls join their mother buying grapes for New Year's Eve in a market in Valencia, Spain. In Spain and Portugal, it is traditional to eat 12 grapes at midnight on New Year's Eve for good luck in the new year.

celebrate the holiday outdoors in town squares, drinking vodka and dancing until the early hours of the morning. Younger people will hike out to the mountains and spend the holiday together in a chapel or small hotel known as a "hostel."

Polish people start preparing for New Year long before it occurs. They buy new clothes to celebrate the holiday and try to get invitations to the fanciest and best parties. When the holiday time arrives, people celebrate with a huge bonfire and cheer in the new year.

Eating 12 Grapes for Good Luck in Portugal

The people of Portugal have a tradition of eating 12 grapes as the clock strikes midnight on New Year's Eve. The 12 grapes are thought to bring 12 months of good luck and happiness. There is much laughter as people gulp down their grapes, trying to consume all of them before the final stroke of midnight.

For this national holiday Portuguese children also walk from house to house, singing songs such as "Blonde Parrot" ("Papagaio Lorio"), "Butterfly" ("Borboleta"), and "Catrina's Little Doves" ("As Pombinhas da Catrina"), and receiving small treats. Businesses and schools are closed, so everyone has a day for leisure and parties with family and friends.

Burning a Straw Puppet in Romania

In southeastern Europe along the Black Sea lies the country of Romania. There New Year's celebrations extend from December 31 to January 2. The first two days in January are public holidays. New Year's Eve is usu-

Romanians dance wearing bear furs during New Year's rituals in a town in Romania on December 31. In a pre-Christian rural tradition, dancers wearing colored costumes or animal furs tour from house to house in villages, singing and dancing to ward off evil.

ally spent with family and friends. On this day, as in the United States, a new baby symbolizes the new year and the figure of an elderly person stands for the end of the old year.

In Romania, New Year's Eve traditions include the burning of Jack Straw. This is a puppet figure that is dragged through the streets and then burned to drive out any bad luck left over from the year that is ending. It is also traditional to celebrate with songs and dances. The words of the songs express the Romanians' desire for health, happiness, good weather, and abundant crops. January 1 is known as *Anul Nou*, or New Year.

A Beloved Holiday in Russia

The political body known as the Soviet Union gradually emerged after the four years of civil war that followed the Russian Revolution of 1917. The revolution was the result of rebellion against the autocracy that had ruled Russia for hundreds of years. Under the autocratic system, the lower classes,

Foresters use sleighs to transport fir trees they cut in a forest near Moscow. Russians celebrate New Year much the way Westerners celebrate Christmas. Russians decorate their homes with freshly cut fir trees for New Year.

peasants, and workers endured difficult conditions such as food shortages, lack of drinkable water, and overcrowding, while their leader, the tsar, seemed unaware or unconcerned about their plight. As conditions got worse, a series of smaller rebellions escalated into revolution, which resulted in the death of the tsar, his family, and the other leaders who had been in power.

The Union of Socialist Soviet Republics (USSR) was formed in 1922 from a group of republics, the largest of which was Russia, so it was often referred to by that name. The Communist Party was in charge of the government. The communists argued that a one-party system was necessary to restore order and to restore the economy. In the mid 1980s, however, belief in the power of communism to create a desirable way of life had crumbled. Under communism, practicing religion was forbidden. The communists considered it superstition, and tried to eliminate it through ridicule, repression, and an emphasis on science. In 1991, the Soviet Union was officially dissolved.

Despite no longer being part of the USSR, the country of Russia is still one of the largest in the world. There are two major religions in Russia today: Russian Orthodox (Christians) and Islam (Muslims). In Russia New Year's celebrations last for three days—from December 31 to January 2. Because of its long history as a communist country, these

New Year's celebrations in Russia are often bigger and more important than those at Christmas. Instead of eliminating the customs they loved during communist rule, the Russians turned them into secular, or non-religious, festivities held on New Year. Many Russians decorate fir trees and put gifts under them on New Year's Eve. Russian children excitedly await the arrival of Grandfather Frost (Dyed Moroz, Russia's version of Santa Claus) and the Snow Maiden (Snyegurochka). They believe that these two figures are the ones who leave them presents. There are holiday celebrations both in school and at home.

To celebrate the New Year's holidays, Russians cook a special meal. This usually includes caviar (fish eggs), some smoked fish such as herring or cod, and a variety of meats such as bacon, sausage, and duck. Many kinds of sweets are made for this gathering, especially *babka*, a yeast cake, and *kulich*. *Kulich* is a special fruit bread that has three layers. To the Russians, the three layers are a symbol of the Christian Trinity: God the Father, Jesus the Son, and the Holy Ghost. Some families also enjoy a delicious *tvorok*-and-raisin pie (*tvorok* resembles cheesecake filling).

Late on New Year's Eve, the chimes ring in the world-famous landmark known as Red Square in Moscow, Russia's largest city and capital. When the main clock strikes midnight in the government center (the Kremlin), people toast each other with champagne and officially usher in the new year. This is the time when Russians make their New Year's resolutions. Both January 1 and January 2 are holidays, with schools and offices closed.

A Full Stomach and a Heavy Wallet in Spain

Like their Portuguese neighbors, Spaniards also share the custom of eating 12 grapes at the start of a new year. The Spaniards enjoy fireworks with many of their festivals, and New Year's Eve is no exception. In Spain fireworks are called *fuegos artificales*, which translates as "artificial fires."

Movies and Theater Performances Pause at Midnight in Spain

When the clocks in Spain strike midnight on New Year's Eve, movies and live theater performances stop. This is done so that the actors and audience members can eat their 12 grapes for luck.

Since the Spanish regularly stay up late (dinner is typically served about 9 P.M.), the fireworks may not begin until midnight. New Year's Eve is known as Noche Vieja, or the Old Night. People often drink to the new year with a sparkling white wine called Cava.

By tradition, Spaniards believe that what happens to them on New Year's Day indicates what will happen during the coming year. Some may deliberately place money in their pockets on New Year, for example, in the belief that it will help them earn a lot of money during the year. If they eat well on New Year, it means they will not go hungry during the coming 12 months. On the other hand, not having money on January 1 is a bad omen for the rest of the year.

Two New Years in Switzerland

In Switzerland, the people celebrate Gregorian New Year's Eve and Day (December 31 and January 1). In addition, those who follow the Julian calendar (including certain Swiss Protestant churches and many Eastern Orthodox churches) celebrate January 13 as both New Year's and Saint Sylvester's Day. The Swiss say that letting a drop of cream fall to the floor on New Year will bring good luck. Located in central Europe, Switzerland features a culture that is greatly influenced by its neighbors Germany, France, and Italy, with the result that it boasts three official languages—German, French, and Italian. Because of these outside influences Switzerland does not have a centralized idea of a New Year's celebration so much as it adopts the traditions of its border countries. One may eat French foods such as foie gras

Dressed in pine tree branches and equipped with big cowbells, Silvesterkläuse (New Year's Clauses) walk through the snow-covered countryside of a village in Switzerland. Following an old tradition, they offer their best wishes for the new year (observed in mid January according to the Julian calendar) to the citizens of the region. After their performance of singing and dancing, the Silvesterkläuse receive food, hot drinks, or money.

and drink champagne in one region, watch a German television broadcast in another, and sing traditional Italian folk songs in a third.

The All-Important First Guest in the United Kingdom and Ireland

The United Kingdom, although a nation of islands, is also part of western Europe. Lying between the North Atlantic and the North Sea, the United Kingdom is just across the English Channel from France. The islands of the United Kingdom include England, Scotland, Wales, and Northern Ireland. The Republic of Ireland is an independent country whose capital is Dublin.

First-Footers in England

In Great Britain's capital of London, the British gather to hear the chimes of Big Ben, the world's largest four-faced chiming clock, strike midnight on New Year's Eve. Then they cheer for the coming new year and sing an old Scottish song, "Auld Lang Syne," which is sung on New Year in several English-speaking parts of the world.

Singing "Auld Lang Syne"

Many people in English-speaking parts of the world usher in the New Year by singing "Auld Lang Syne." Loosely translated, the title means "Long, long ago." The song was originally written by the famous Scottish poet Robert Burns (1759-1796), though other versions exist. Here is the first verse and chorus.

Should auld acquaintance be forgot,
And ne'er brought to mind?
Should auld acquaintance be forgot,
And days of auld lang syne.

For auld lang syne, my dear,
For auld lang syne,
We'll take a cup of kindness yet,
For auld lang syne!

(Quiller-Couch 1919)

The British also believe in the tradition of the first-footer. This means that the ideal person to be the first to enter their house on New Year's Day would be a good-looking, dark-haired young man with pockets full of salt, money, bread, and coal. In addition to these traditional gifts, he often brings some whiskey to share and toast the new year. The young man prepares these items beforehand and takes them to a neighboring home just after the stroke of midnight. His visit ensures good luck for the family. He may first-foot his own home provided he is not present in the house at midnight. It is considered bad luck for the first visitor to be a woman, or any person with red hair (what they call "ginger-haired").

In the Front Door and Out the Back Door in Ireland

As midnight strikes on New Year's Eve in the independent country of Ireland, which includes five-sixths of the island (the other sixth of the island is Northern Ireland, which is part of the United Kingdom), families walk in the front doors of their homes and right out the back. This is done in order to bring good luck. Many of the Irish will keep some of the special raisin, currant, and caraway seed bread (known as Irish soda bread) they made for Christmas and use it as part of an Irish tradition. They bang the bread on the doors and windows to drive out bad spirits and keep good spirits in. On New Year's Day, another tradition is to take a very brief swim in the cold sea. This tradition has spread to a variety of other places, including the United States, where the people who participate are part of groups usually called "polar bear clubs." Members put on their bathing suits and plunge into local icy waters, quickly emerging gasping for breath and laughing. Some groups use these occasions to raise money for a favorite charity.

There are many Irish superstitions associated with New Year's Eve and New Year's Day. One says that if a person is wearing shoes with holes in them at this time, he or she will have money problems in the coming year. Another says people should not wash any clothes on New Year. If they do, draining out the dirty water will most likely bring them bad luck.

Celebrating Hogmanay in Scotland

In Scotland, part of the United Kingdom, people celebrate the new year with traditional foods such as shortbread, black buns, oatcakes, wine, whiskey, and cheese. New Year's Eve is known as Hogmanay. There are a number

Men in Viking costumes take part in the torchlight procession in Edinburgh, Scotland, which marks the start of the Hogmanay celebrations.

of theories as to where the name comes from; one source seems to be the French "Homme est né" or "Man is born."

It is only in recent years that Hogmanay has been celebrated on a large scale: The first event of its kind was at "Summit in the City" in 1992 when Scotland's capital, Edinburgh, hosted the European Union Heads of State conference. This Hogmanay festival was so successful that similar events have sprung up throughout Scotland, turning it into a countrywide street party with dancing, music, fireworks, and bonfires. For those who live far from the city, or who don't like crowds, there are always smaller, local parties they can attend.

One reason that Hogmanay has become such a jubilant celebration may be due to the fact that Christmas celebrations were essentially banned in Scotland for nearly 400 years—from the end of the 17th century to the 1950s. During a period of religious upheaval known as the Protestant Reformation, the Protestant Church in Scotland decided that people had gotten too far away from the most important elements of their religion. They wanted to "purify" their church and also to separate from anything that might be considered Catholic, so they banned Christmas celebrations. Many Scots had to work during Christmas, therefore New Year became the time to celebrate the winter solstice, hold parties, and exchange gifts with family and friends.

New Year's revelers participate in the Hogmanay celebrations in Edinburgh, Scotland, on December 31.

The Scots share the tradition of the first-footer with the English, but they also have some customs that are unique. One example of a local Hogmanay custom takes place in Stonehaven, Kincardineshire, in northeast Scotland. Here people use chicken wire, tar, paper, and other flammable materials to make giant spheres that weigh up to 20 pounds each. After they are attached to a wire or chain, the balls are set on fire, then swung around by locals as they march up and down the High Street. The origin of this custom is believed to come from pre-Christian rituals in which fire represented the power of the Sun.

In Allendale, Scotland, a procession of people known as *guisers* parade down the street with burning tar barrels balanced on their heads. *Guiser* is an old folk term that comes from *guise* (as in *disguise*), meaning anyone who takes on a different form or appearance. Like kids dressing up for Halloween, the fun comes in the costumes. January 2 is a holiday in Scotland in addition to the first day of the year. It gives everyone time to recover from all the merrymaking.

Latin America and the Caribbean

According to the United Nations, Latin America includes South America, Central America, Mexico, and the islands in the Caribbean, such as Puerto Rico, Aruba, and Jamaica. The background of the many peoples who have come to Latin America throughout the years or who are indigenous, that is, native inhabitants, have contributed to the complex blending of cultures, customs, and races that characterizes the region. This large influx of immigrant peoples, including French, German, Scottish, Irish, Portuguese, Scandinavian, Swiss, English, Welsh, Japanese, Korean, Vietnamese, Laotian, Chinese, Ashkenazi and Sephardic Jews, Greeks, Serbians, and others, ensures a diversity of New Year's Eve and New Year's Day celebrations.

Common Observances

At the Stroke of Midnight

Despite the broad range of ethnic groups assembled in Latin America, the majority of them celebrate New Year according to the Gregorian calendar (December 31/January 1). Of course many people in the region celebrate multiple New Year—pockets of Asians who observe Chinese New Year, Muslims who follow the calendar of Islam, and Jews who observe Rosh Hashanah as New Year. Sometimes people prefer to observe a religious New Year according to their culture's calendar, but take part in festivities on December 31 in the spirit of public celebration. Since most Latin American countries are either located in the Southern Hemisphere, or close to the equator, the weather is usually the opposite from what North Americans experience on New Year. Of course in mountainous areas such as the Andes, the high altitude keeps the climate cool or cold all year round.

The ritual of eating 12 grapes at midnight on New Year's Eve takes place in the Spanish- and Portuguese-speaking countries of Latin America just as it does in Spain and Portugal. People usually prepare 12 wishes before the clock begins to strike midnight. With each strike of the clock, they are supposed to eat a grape and silently make one of their wishes.

Describing the ritual is simpler than doing it—it is easy to get flustered trying to synchronize swallowing the grapes, listening to the clock, and making the wishes. In some countries, such as Venezuela, it is customary to write wishes down and then burn the list. This ritual is supposed to make the wishes come true.

Colored Underwear for Luck

In Latin America, particularly in countries that border the Caribbean, many people wear yellow underwear on New Year's Eve to bring them good luck. In some countries, it is best to acquire the underwear as a gift. Often friends will go out in the month before New Year to buy each other yellow underwear, just to be sure they do not have to buy their own. A few places also believe the greatest luck comes to those who wear the underwear inside out or backward, even though no one but the wearer knows.

Booths selling *moda amarilla* (yellow fashion) pop up in the weeks preceding New Year, in department stores, clothing stores, and even on

A man walks by a display of traditional puppets made of straw and dressed in old clothes in a town in Colombia. Colombians traditionally make these straw puppets to be burned on New Year's Eve to erase the bad things that happened the previous year.

Masks representing Ecuadorean politicians are waiting to be burned on New Year's Eve. Ecuadorians traditionally burn these straw figures representing people that have been in the news during the year on New Year's Eve.

street corners. Women are more likely to follow this custom than men, but it is considered lucky for both. In Mexico, yellow brings prosperity and luck, but to attract love, red underwear should be worn.

Another fun Latin American custom is to pack a suitcase and carry it for a short walk, setting out right after midnight. This practice is for those who want to travel during the coming year. Participants need only walk a short distance, but since the walk should come immediately after eating the 12 grapes, the time around midnight can be rather frantic, especially for those who are new to the experience. To make the situation even more confusing, in many places in Latin America laws restricting private fireworks are ignored during New Year. As a result, the deafening sound of exploding firecrackers adds to the chaos and hilarity as people madly gulp down grapes, grab their suitcases, and dash out into the streets, happy in the knowledge that under their regular clothes are concealed their lucky yellow underwear turned inside out!

A Symbolic Funeral for the Old Year

Many Latin Americans share the custom of getting rid of the *año viejo* (the old year). In countries such as Mexico, Colombia, Venezuela, and Ecuador, people stuff firecrackers, paper, and wood into dummies dressed up in old clothes to symbolize the old year. In Ecuador the dummies are often made to look like people in the news or local politicians who are unpopular. Some people also traditionally dress in black and pretend they

A member of a Junkanoo group dances in the street in Nassau, Bahamas, during the Junkanoo Parade to celebrate New Year. The man's costume and his group's theme honor the freedom of the formerly enslaved and the U.S. civil rights movement. The annual street festival draws thousands of spectators on New Year's Eve.

are widows. They ask for money to help arrange a funeral for the dummy. At midnight, the dummies are put outside and burned, symbolizing the death of the old year and the hope that the new year will bring good fortune. Once the flames hit the firecrackers placed nearby, the old year explodes.

Unique Traditions and Customs

Good Luck Musicians in Aruba

In Aruba, an island of the Caribbean situated north of Venezuela, a special group of musicians known as *dande* or *dandee* have become an essential part of the year-end celebrations. During New Year's festivities, *dande* go from house to house, singing and wishing people good luck in the coming year. This tradition is so strong that some fear they will have bad luck if they are not visited by the *dande*.

Junkanoo in the Bahamas

New Year's Day is one of the most widely celebrated holidays in the Caribbean, especially the Bahamas. On this day people wear masks and costumes and dance at big street parties in a celebration known as *junkanoo*. Music is a big part of life in the Bahamas and the New Year's celebration is no exception.

On New Year's Day, there is a huge parade in the capital of Nassau. People celebrate with parties, family gatherings, and by wearing colorful masks and costumes. In the early hours of morning, junkanoo bands, playing a unique blend of European and African rhythms, fill the streets. Playing from about 2 A.M. to 8 A.M., they bring in the new year with the sounds of singing, cowbells, whistles, horns, and drums. People dress in elaborate costumes and some walk on stilts. Fireworks are also included. The whole parade route is one big loud party.

Good Luck Dolls in Bolivia

The people of Bolivia celebrate only three national holidays. These are New Year's Day (January 1), Labor Day (May 1), and Independence Day (August 6). With only three national holidays, each one is very important. In Bolivia, people craft beautiful handmade dolls before the New Year's celebrations. These are fashioned out of straw or wood and are in the image of Ekeko, the god of abundance, who is believed to fulfill a family's material needs when summoned. People hang the dolls outside of their homes to bring good luck in the coming year.

Fireworks and a Gift to the Goddess in Brazil

Few—if any—countries can throw parties to match those of Brazil. Best known for its Carnival celebrations in February or March, the New Year's celebrations are also spectacular.

A man throws talcum powder to an image of Yemaja, the sea goddess in Rio de Janeiro, Brazil. It is a Brazilian New Year's Eve tradition to make an offering to the goddess, an Afro-Brazilian ritual to ask for a good new year.

A woman places flowers around candles on Copacabana beach in Rio de Janeiro, Brazil. It is a Brazilian New Year's Eve tradition to make an offering to the goddess of the sea, Yemaja.

For New Year, more than 2 million people gather from around the world to party in Rio de Janeiro, the capital. People dress in white for good luck. There are concerts, parties, music, and dancing on a large scale. The fireworks display in Rio de Janeiro begins at midnight. It ranks as one of the best and most famous in the entire world.

For those who can tear themselves away from the parties, there is a different kind of ritual observed in Rio on New Year's Eve that focuses on Yemaja (or Iemanja), the goddess of the water and fish. Enslaved persons who came from Yorubaland in southwestern Nigeria, Africa, brought their reverence for Yemaja to Brazil. She is known by many different names with many different spellings in various countries of the Caribbean, because African traditions were typically communicated orally and not written. The festival is observed in the city of Salvador on February 2, but in Rio de Janeiro, the night of December 31 is the time to honor her.

The ceremony in Brazil began in 1923, when a group of fishermen asked for her help during a particularly bad fishing season. Today hundreds of people go down to the beach dressed in white to offer her gifts, flowers, perfume, and rice. These offerings are placed in little boats and rowed out to sea by local fishermen, or else tossed directly into the water. This joyful ceremony is a way of thanking her for the blessings of the past year while requesting her favors in the year to come. Singing, chanting, and musical accompaniment form a backdrop to the ceremony. Young and old alike carry candles lit in her honor, filling the beaches with multitudes of dancing lights.

According to legend, Yemaja is vain and beautiful, which is why gifts of mirrors, jewelry, combs, and makeup appear in many of the offerings. She is sometimes pictured as a mermaid, and her image shows up throughout seacoast towns. Some people spend weeks preparing and decorating the baskets that they will offer her, whereas others create simpler collections of items. The belief is that if an offering sinks, it means the goddess has accepted it, and will protect the person who offered it through the year.

In the city of Salvador, there is a different religious festival celebrated on January 1. A procession of boats carries a statue of Jesus from Salvador's main harbor to the Boa Viagem beach. Taking part in this procession is believed to safeguard local sailors from the threat of drowning. In Salvador, offerings to Yemaja take place in the following month.

Three Times the Bang in Chile

In Chile people eat lentils because they are supposed to represent good luck, financial abundance, and fertility. But at a typical New Year's party one is more likely to find empanadas (pastries stuffed with seasoned meat and vegetables), roasted or grilled meats, several salads, and a variety of puddings for

Fireworks explode over Santiago, Chile, during the New Year's celebrations on January 1.

Famous Cable Cars in Chile

Visitors who go to Valparaíso for the New Year's fireworks should definitely make time to see the city during daylight hours as well. In 1996, the World Monuments' Fund declared the city's unusual system of cable cars one of the world's 100 most endangered historical treasures. The system in which cable cars are pulled up a steep incline is known as a funicular elevator or railway. In Valparaíso, the funicular elevators carry people between the upper and lower portions of the city. In 1998, supporters of the cable cars convinced the Chilean government to apply to UNESCO (United Nations Educational Scientific, and Cultural Organization) for world heritage status for Valparaíso. This would be a great boost for tourism, the economy, and national pride.

dessert. Valparaíso, a major city in Chile, combines forces with two other cities to put on an amazing display of fireworks at midnight on New Year's Eve. Known as "Fireworks by the Sea," the event is organized by a fireworks expert and requires approximately 20 tons of fireworks in a colorful spectacle that lasts about 25 minutes. The fireworks are set off in seven locations, extending along more than 15 miles of coastline, with the result that everyone present gets to enjoy not only the display closest to them, but the unforgettable sight of the other displays stretching out along the shore.

New Year's Takeover in Cuba

Cuba, an island located quite close to the coast of Florida, has experienced great political upheaval during the last century. Although it obtained its independence from Spain, it still struggled with economic difficulties and leaders who did not help the people they were supposed to serve. Like so many other Latin American countries, Cuba also became the new home of many immigrants from other countries. Some, such as enslaved Africans, experienced racism even after they had officially been freed. Others, such as the many Spaniards who arrived hoping they could find more opportunities than in their country of origin, discovered that Cuba was not the place they had imagined. Hope turned to disappointment, once it was clear that obtaining independence was not going to solve

Cuba's problems. The leadership of the new republic never fulfilled its promise. Eventually, Cuba became controlled by a series of dictators, each no better than the previous one.

After more than 50 years of economic disasters, violence in the streets, a lack of basic necessities, and being terrorized by gangsters as well as by police, many Cubans viewed Fidel Castro's revolution with hope. On January 1 of 1959, Fidel Castro overthrew the military dictator Fulgencio Batista, seized control of the country, and instituted a government based on communist principles modeled on the former Soviet Union. As a result, January 1 is celebrated in Cuba as Liberation Day, not New Year's Day. Military parades and celebrations are held across the country to commemorate this historical event. Decorations fill the streets and towns and cities sponsor concerts and other cultural events.

How history will evaluate Castro's presidency of Cuba remains to be seen. While in 2007–2008 Cuba ranked 51 out of 177 countries on the United Nations' human development index, which measures health, education, and living standards, Castro's government has also committed appalling human rights violations and ruthlessly silenced any opposition.

Music and Merriment in Jamaica

Music and dancing are also essential ingredients for New Year in other parts of the Caribbean. Jamaican music includes calypso, reggae, *soca*, and steel bands. Calypso began as a way for enslaved people to send messages to each other as they worked in the fields. This was their only means of communication because they were required to work in silence. Calypso combined a mix of sounds that came from many African peoples. Reggae began in Jamaica and is based on Jamaican music from the 1950s. *Soca*

How Steel Drums Are Made

Although the structure of a steel drum seems quite simple, making one is much more difficult than it looks. For example, the process of pounding out the bottom of the barrel with a 40-pound sledgehammer can take up to five hours of hammering. Bands usually find a panmaker whose work they respect, and then hire that person to make all their drums. Finished drums usually start at a price of $750.

rhythms are a blend of slower beats from soul music and quick ones from calypso.

Many visitors also associate the Caribbean with the unique sound of a steel drum band. Although the Trinidadians (people of Trinidad) are given credit for inventing the first steel drums, steel drum music has spread to other islands of the Caribbean, as well as many other locations around the world. Sometimes the number of steel band musicians is so great the band is more like an orchestra. Usually associated with Carnival, steel band music is also a common element of New Year's celebrations, especially in Jamaica, Trinidad, and Tobago.

Steel drums (also called pans) are a brilliant example of recycling: The bottom of an empty 55-gallon oil drum is hammered until it stretches into a dish shape. The metal must stretch without becoming deformed. Then, the panmaker uses a tuning device to adjust the sound. Finally, the pan is painted bright colors, and then retuned to adjust for changes made by the paint. The musician strikes the pan on different areas to achieve different notes.

Coming Full Circle: Mayan New Year in Mexico and Guatemala

The Mayan peoples of Guatemala and Mexico currently speak more than 30 Mayan languages. One out of eight Maya live in the United States today. Because the Mayan calendar follows a 260-day cycle, the date for New Year in relation to the Gregorian calendar changes from year to year. In Mayan, New Year is called Wajxaqib' B'at'z.

Whereas typically the Gregorian calendar emphasizes releasing the old year and facing the new, the Mayan emphasis is on recognizing that life has come full circle at the end of the year. As in Western culture, it is customary to get together with family and community members during New Year and enjoy a period of renewal. The Mayan celebration of the new year combines religious and nonreligious elements, moments of quiet contemplation, as well as abundant feasts and colorful processions. As in so many other cultures, the first step is to prepare for the coming year by cleaning the household and places of worship. On New Year's Day itself, the Maya light bonfires with the belief that the flames will scare off evil spirits.

To mark the New Year, sacred rituals also take place in Mayan communities across Guatemala and Mexico, performed by the Mayan priests or holy people, who are called *aki jab*. This is also the time during which new priests are initiated into their role as servants of the community. In addition to the spiritual elements of their New Year's celebrations, the Maya repaint the doorways of their homes in whimsical colors and decorate with bright tapestries and mats.

Let's Dance in Paraguay!

At one time, Paraguay, a land-locked country in South America, was referred to as "South America's empty quarter." Its isolation from the rest of its neighbors stemmed from a series of dictatorships that began shortly after its independence from Spain in 1811. The dictator José Gaspar Rodríguez de Francia nicknamed "El Supremo," who controlled Paraguay from 1814 until 1840, closed Paraguay's borders to foreigners. Trade with the outside world was only allowed in designated locations by merchants who had been approved by the government. Although "El Supremo" died in 1840, he was followed by other dictators, including one who instituted a police state that lasted 35 years.

Given the frequent instability of its government; a disastrous war against Uruguay, Argentina, and Brazil; and the numerous human rights violations and corrupt acts committed by successive leaders, Paraguay was long considered a place to avoid. It has only been since the mid-1990s that Paraguay has consciously begun to transform itself. The country

Dancing with Bottles on One's Head

Paraguay's *danza* or *baile de la botella,* which is a variation on a dance called the *galopa* (*galopar* means "to gallop"), is an impressive display of balance and the ability to move while keeping one's head still. In the dance, which is only performed by women, a group of dancers move around a central dancer who places a jar or bottle on her head. She continues to dance while more bottles or jars are stacked on top of those already carefully balanced. As the tower of bottles gets higher and higher, someone must stand on a ladder to add another one. Sometimes a dancer can dance with as many as 14 bottles on her head, without letting any of them fall.

now actively welcomes visitors and is trying to overcome its long years of isolation, while simultaneously trying to address such issues as health concerns and economic reforms.

One reason to visit Paraguay is that in this country people like to dance their way into the new year. No fiesta in Paraguay can be considered a success if dancing is not included. Town halls and wealthy homes typically include a tile or clay floor on which people can dance, frequently barefoot. Paraguayan music closely resembles European dance music. As a result, Paraguayan dances are similar to polka, waltz, or tango. Native dances are often accompanied by a couple of guitars and a small harp called an *arpa*.

On January 1, Paraguayans rearrange the nativity scenes (scenes of the birth of Jesus) that they placed in their homes before Christmas and begin to call Jesus *niño del año buevo:* "the baby of the new year." (Before January 1, Jesus is called *niño de la navidad,* "the baby of Christmas).￼" New Year's Eve and New Year's Day festivities are held throughout the country with music and parties. In addition to the festivities held at hotels and homes, river cruises are a popular way to celebrate the new year. Paraguay has some impressive waterways, and these are ideal for a floating party, complete with gourmet food, a band to dance to, and constantly changing scenery. The food served is often international in flavor, thus honoring the blend of European and indigenous cultures in Paraguayan history, and includes smoked meats, sushi, and decorated ham.

Middle East

As a region, the Middle East is partially a political construction of the 19th century, though it has always been a distinct crossroad of cultures. The major religions of Judaism, Christianity, and Islam all began in the Middle East, and share some common roots in the region's history. In major metropolitan areas such as Dubai, New Year is a large, Western-style celebration featuring fireworks, dancing, and public concerts. Smaller cities and towns mark the new year with quieter but no less festive events such as gathering family and friends together at local bars and cafés.

Saint Basil in Cyprus

In Cyprus, a Mediterranean island, children dress as Father Christmas and sing traditional songs on New Year's Eve. It is customary for families to make a cake with a coin hidden in it for the holiday. Whoever receives the piece of cake with the coin in it is guaranteed good luck in the coming year. The same custom prevails in Greece.

About three quarters of Cypriots are Greek Orthodox. For those who are Greek Orthodox, January 1 is mainly celebrated as Saint Basil's Day. Saint Basil—also known as Basil the Great—is very important to the Greek Orthodox church. Many of his teachings and rules are still central to the church's beliefs. As a young, well-educated man, Basil was such a great speaker that he began to take pride in his ability. When he saw that he was focusing more on his own accomplishments than on teaching others about God, he decided that his love for God was more important than his success as a speaker. He sold all that he owned and became a monk. He was known for his charity and generosity, especially to the poor and needy. That is why on Cyprus and in Greece, gifts are usually given on this day instead of on Christmas.

A Quiet Holiday in Turkey

Turkey is a country located between southeastern Europe and southwestern Asia. Virtually all of its citizens are Muslims. Generally the public New Year's holiday is celebrated as a day of rest. According to custom, Turkish families spend New Year's Eve getting together with family and friends for a special dinner. Today, however, there are some Turks who hold outdoor parties and enjoy a nighttime display of fireworks.

North America

From the famous dropping of the ball in Times Square, New York City, to the close of the financial year in Western economies, the new year arrives forcefully in North America. New Year's Eve is a time for parties with family and friends. New Year is also a time of reflection, especially on the day following all the hooplah—New Year's Day. On this day almost all businesses (except restaurants serving special brunches) close, and people think back on the year and often rededicate themselves to the year ahead.

New Year in Canada

People in Canada celebrate New Year's Eve and New Year's Day with family and friends. As is the custom in the United States, many people make resolutions—or set goals—for how they want to improve themselves in the coming year. They hold parties and enjoy watching fireworks and using noisemakers at the moment a new year begins.

The more rural areas of Canada have more specific and localized traditions. For instance, in the northern provinces ice fishing is a popular way to spend New Year's Eve. First-footer traditions, like those in the United Kingdom, are also very popular. Bowls of black-eyed pea soup are consumed, gifts are exchanged, and loud claps and cheers welcome the new year. On New Year's Day, hearty celebrants keep up the tradition of the "polar bear" swim. In the early hours of the morning they plunge into frigid waters as a means of reawakening their bodies and minds for the new year.

Vancouver (18.2 percent) and Toronto (9.6 percent) have large Chinese-Canadian populations, and Chinese New Year is celebrated in both cities. In Vancouver, the Spring Parade is held in Chinatown on the first Sunday of Lunar New Year.

Light in the Cold Climate of Greenland

Greenland, a country in North America, is part of the kingdom of Denmark. The major languages spoken there are Greenlandic (also called East Inuit), Danish, and English. Greenland is the largest island in the world, with a coastline about the length of the equator. Nonetheless, there are only about 60,000 people in all of Greenland. For the most part, the people live in small areas along the Atlantic Coast or in the capital

Children reach out and touch a Chinese lion head during the Chinese New Year parade in Vancouver, Canada.

city of Nuuk. The harsh climate—not to mention the country's ice cap—keeps Greenland's population low. The climate of this country ranges from arctic to subarctic, with frigid winters and cool summers.

For the people of Greenland, New Year's celebrations (on December 31 and January 1) provide a much-needed break in a land that endures such long and dark winters. In the countryside, peoples' spirits are high on New Year's Eve and many play pranks on each other. Throughout the country celebrations also include dancing, fireworks, and concerts that last all night. As in Denmark, an old belief says that finding broken dishes at one's door will bring good luck, which explains why people in Greenland save their broken dishes throughout the year. At the new year, it is customary to leave them in front of friends' front doors.

Just as in most countries of the world, the people in Greenland like to set aside New Year's Eve and New Year's Day for parties with their family and friends. On New Year's Eve, it is common for the people of Greenland to

Celebrating New Year Twice in Greenland

Since Greenland is part of the kingdom of Denmark it celebrates the new year twice—first at 8 P.M. because there is a four-hour difference between Denmark and Greenland—and then at midnight, Greenland time.

hold fireworks celebrations and to ring church bells to usher in the new year. On New Year's Day, the queen of Denmark and other leaders of the country make speeches that are broadcast over Greenland radio and television.

United States: Having a Ball in Times Square

On December 31, 1904, the owner of the *New York Times* threw a huge party in Times Square in New York City. The festivities lasted all day and culminated in a fireworks display. This first celebration led to the now world-

The highlight of the Times Square festivities in New York City is a huge lit crystal ball that slowly drops to mark the final countdown to midnight. A new Times Square crystal ball was inaugurated in 2007. The new ball is more than twice as bright as its predecessor with enhanced color capabilities and state-of-the-art LED lighting effects. The new ball marked the 100th anniversary celebration of the Times Square ball.

famous tradition of lowering a ball in Times Square to signal the new year. Today, people travel from around the United States and the globe to see the ball drop in person. To get the best view possible, revelers arrive hours before midnight and spend the day waiting in the cold. Most people in the United States, however, watch the ball drop on television, where they can enjoy the celebrity hosts and concerts from the comfort of home.

In recent years, many cities in the United States as well as in Canada have started holding "First Night" festivals. First Night celebrations are intended for enjoyment by people of all ages. The events usually include such attractions as ice sculptures, nighttime parades, artists' displays, dancing, singing, and eating holiday foods, especially soups and hot drinks such as mulled cider. First Night was begun as a safe way to have fun on New Year's Eve without the presence of alcohol, so alcohol is not permitted. Most events are scheduled from the early afternoon to late evening of the day before New Year's Day so that children can celebrate with their parents. Started in Boston in 1976, this new tradition provides a way for families and communities from the whole area to come together and enjoy the holiday.

A New Year's reveler peers out from his costume at the beginning of the annual First Night Parade in Boston on December 31. Nearly a million people participate in the festivities in Boston to welcome the new year.

Oceania

Oceania is the name of the region that encompasses many island countries located in the Pacific Ocean. There are more than 10,000 islands in this region. They vary in size from very tiny islands to the sprawling island continent of Australia. Most people who live in Oceania observe the Gregorian (December 31/January 1) New Year's holiday. Because the region is in the Southern Hemisphere, New Year is summertime for them. Warm weather outdoor activities are usually part of their celebrations.

New Year in Australia

Every New Year's Day the small town of Pine Creek, located in the Northern Territories, sponsors a wild boar and wild cat hunt. The hunter who kills the most animals is awarded a cash prize at a New Year's party. Organizers of the hunt argue that it is necessary to reduce the overpopulation of wild boars and the environmental impact of feral cats that prey on other animals in that portion of Australia. Nevertheless, the competition draws yearly protest from the Royal Society for Prevention of Cruelty to Animals, undoubtedly because hunters are allowed to use any means available to kill the animals, including hitting them with cars and blowing them up with dynamite.

Because Australia is located in the Southern Hemisphere, Australians have become accustomed to celebrating New Year during their summer season. On January 1, while Aussie beaches are crowded with people swimming, surfing, and enjoying picnics, in the Northern Hemisphere, even Polar Bear Club members wouldn't dream of spending more than a few minutes in the water.

The Sky Tower in Auckland, New Zealand, explodes in a flurry of fireworks at the stroke of midnight on January 1.

All the major cities of Australia have fireworks to mark the beginning of the new year, but the two largest cities, Sydney and Melbourne, outdo themselves with their firework displays on New Year's Eve. In Melbourne, an average number of 500,000 watch the pyrotechnic display. Sydney, however, tops that by putting on what is sometimes the largest firework display in the world. Sydney typically chooses a different theme each year, which is played out in a variety of effects and dazzling light shows on the Sydney Harbor Bridge.

During the New Year's Eve celebrating the end of 2007 and the beginning of 2008, the fireworks were launched from 7 barges in the harbor, 10 buildings in the city, the Sydney Harbor Bridge, and a nearby highway. The pyrotechnics stretched across almost 4 miles, and lasted approximately 15 minutes. It was the largest display thus far in Sydney's history.

The Sydney Harbor Bridge is alight with fireworks to welcome in the New Year in Sydney, Australia.

Communal Holiday in Kiribati

The small country of Kiribati is located in Micronesia (the islands of the West Pacific Ocean east of the Philippines). There are about 100,000 people in Kiribati and most of them are Christian. For New Year, the I-Kiribati (the citizens of this country) gather in meetinghouses called *maneabas* to share holiday meals, sing, give speeches, and play games. When midnight strikes, they say goodbye to the old year, welcome the new one, and pray together. People sing folk songs in the traditional Kiribati style—a mixture of guitar, chanting, and rhythmic percussion—and dance along with outstretched arms and broad, swooping movements.

First to Greet Each New Year in Tonga

Tonga is a group of islands in the South Pacific Ocean situated two-thirds of the way between Hawaii and New Zealand. Because of its location just to the west of the International Date Line, Tonga is the first nation to see the Sun rise each day and thus the first to see every new year. The New Year's festivities in Tonga are of major importance. January 1 is an official Tongan holiday, and is called Po Leo on the islands. People celebrate New Year's Eve and Day by hosting parties, holding dances and musical gatherings, and enjoying time with family and friends.

Glossary

ancestors   Relatives of previous generations

archipelago   A group of islands

arctic   Related to the North Pole, or regions close to it

autocracy   A system of government in which one person has all the power

autonomous   Independent

bonfire   A large fire built outdoors

bourgeois   A French word meaning middle class, but usually implying materialistic values

Buddhist   A follower of Buddhism, a religion that originated in Asia from the teachings of Gautama Buddha. Gautama believed that suffering was caused by desire and that freedom from suffering could only be achieved through moral behavior, wisdom, and mental discipline (including meditation)

capitalist   A person who favors an economic system in which individuals and corporations own goods (as opposed to the government), and prices are determined by competition

celestials   Heavenly or mythical beings

communist   A follower of the political and economic theories developed by Karl Marx and Friedrich Engels. Marx and Engels believed that all property should be publicly owned, and a classless society created. Although communism was promoted as a way to free the poor from oppression by the rich, the actual result was that the government had total control and oppressed everyone who opposed it.

couplet   A verse of two lines, usually rhyming

crescendo   A gradual increase in force or intensity

dictator   A ruler who has complete power, often maintaining it through force

drought   A prolonged period of little or no rainfall, especially if it is severe enough to affect crops

ethnic   Referring to a group of people who share the same cultural, tribal, national, linguistic, or religious origins or background

familial   Relating to the family or its members

glutinous   Sticky, glue-like

granules   Small particles

hemisphere   The northern or southern half of Earth as divided along the equator

Hindu   A follower of Hinduism, the dominant religion of India

idealized   Represented as perfect or better than it really is

indigenous   Originating or occurring naturally in a specific place

Islam   The religious faith of Muslims. Muslims believe that Allah is the only God, and Muhammad was his prophet

line of succession   The order that determines who will inherit next

lunar   Related to the Moon

mainland China   The People's Republic of China

monarch   A person who rules a kingdom or empire, often a king or queen

moratorium   To stop or prohibit an activity for a period of time

municipalities   Political units that are self-governed

navigable   A route that is wide or deep enough to allow passage

police state   A political situation in which the government has complete control, and authorizes police (often secret police) to spy on the citizens and act against them without restriction from laws or opposition

propaganda   Biased or misleading information that is used to promote a particular point of view

resolution   To reach a firm decision about

secular   Nonreligious; not connected to a religion

Shinto   A religion native to Japan, which includes worship of nature spirits and one's ancestors. Shinto followers believe that both living and nonliving things have sacred energy

shortbread   A thick cookie made from flour, sugar, and usually a large quantity of butter

solar   Related to the Sun

solilunar   Relating to both the Sun and Moon

subarctic   Colder than arctic

temperate   Having a moderate climate without extreme highs or lows

tropical   A climate with temperatures that do not fall below freezing

typhoon   A hurricane that occurs in the Pacific Ocean, rather than the Atlantic

veneration   Regarding with respect

Bibliography

Buckley, Christopher. "China battles winter weather chaos ahead of holiday," *International Herald Tribune*. Jan 27, 2008. Available online. URL: http://www.iht.com/articles/reuters/2008/01/27/asia/oukwd-uk-china-weather.php. Accessed September 26, 2008.

Kozar, Seanna. "Recreating Chinese New Year on the Internet," American Folklore Society, 1994. Available online. URL: http://jcmc.indiana.edu/vol1/issue2/kozar.html. Accessed January 16, 2008.

Lao Tsu. *Tao Te Ching* translated by Gia-Fu Feng and Jane English. New York: Vintage Books, 1972.

Logan, Christopher. "Paper Decorations for Chinese New Year." Travel in Taiwan. [n.d.] Available online. URL: http://www.sinica.edu.tw/tit/festivals/0297_new-year.html. Accessed January 16, 2009.

Quiller-Couch, Sir Arthur Thomas, ed. *The Oxford Book of English Verse 1250–1900*. Oxford: Clarendon, 1919 {c.1901}; Bartleby.com, 1999. Available online. URL: http://www.bartleby.com/101. Accessed September 26, 2008.

Thich Nhat Hanh. *Old Path White Clouds: Walking in the Footsteps of the Buddha*. Berkeley, Calif.: Parallax Press, 1991.

Walker, John. Calendar Converter. Available online. URL: http://www.fourmilab.ch.documents.calendar. Accessed September 26, 2008.

Further Resources

ᘒᘓ

Books

What You Will See Inside a Hindu Temple. By Mahendra and Vandana Jani. Published in 2005 by SkyLight Paths Publishing, Woodstock, Vt. An attractive and accessible introduction to Hinduism focuses on worship in the temple although it also covers major scriptures, festivals (including New Year), and life events.

The Return of the Light: Twelve Tales from Around the World for the Winter Solstice (Around the World Series). By Carolyn McVickar Edwards. Published in 2003 by Marlowe & Company, Berkeley, Calif. Folktales that offer the reader a glimpse into other cultures as they mark the winter solstice.

In the Light of the Moon: Thirteen Lunar Tales from Around the World Illuminating Life's Mysteries (Around the World Series). By Carolyn McVickar Edwards. Published in 2005 by Marlowe & Company, Berkeley, Calif. International folktales tied together by the universal fascination with the Moon and its cycles.

World Celebrations and Ceremonies–New Year. By Michele Spirn. Published in 1999 by Blackbirch Press, Woodbridge, Conn. Informative and makes the most of every page with a country map for each entry and full-color photos of people celebrating.

Chinese New Year (Images of Asia). By Patricia Bjaaland Welch. Published in 1997 by Oxford University Press, Oxford, England. Easy-to-read explanation of Chinese New Year, plus old and new customs associated with the holiday.

Web Sites

Abya Yala Net. http://abyala.nativeweb.org. A Web site dedicated to dispersing information about indigenous cultures around the world. Includes maps, showing where various groups exist, and many links to further resources.

Calendar Conversion. http://www.fourmilab.ch/documents/calendar. A public-domain Web site that allows people to input dates in one calendar to see the equivalent dates in another calendar. In addition to the more well-known calendars such as the Gregorian, Julian, Islamic, Jewish, and Indian calendars, lesser-known calendars, such as the Mayan calendar and the French Republican Calendar (created during the French Revolution), are included.

China the Beautiful. http://www.chinapage.org. Award-winning bilingual Web site (English/Chinese) consisting of more than 4,000 Web pages dedicated to Chinese culture, including novels, arts, history, literature, poetry, calligraphy, painting, and philosophy. Includes an alphabetical list of topics, links to online dictionaries, explanations of Chinese characters, dates for festival days, and a printable bilingual calendar. For students interested in finding out more about the Chinese Zodiac, this site is a good source. The site is edited by Professor Emeritus Ming L. Pei.

How Steel Drums Are Made. http://www.toucans.net/Toc/makePan.html. A link within a Web site belonging to a popular steel drum band called the Toucans has lots of information and pictures for those interested in finding out more about the history of steel drums, and how they are made. There are also MP3 and video clips of steel drum panmakers and musicians.

Latin American Folk Institute. http://www.lafi.org. Articles related to various aspects of Latin American Folk Art, plus numerous links to specific Latin American arts: music, dance, poetry, painting, etc.

Mystery of the Maya. http://www.civilization.ca/civil/maya. Sponsored by the Canadian Museum of Civilization, this site is in support of the IMAX film, *Mystery of the Maya*. It contains information on Mayan culture, including the Mayan calendar, as well as links to other Maya-related sites.

New Year's Day—History, Traditions, and Customs. http://wilstar/holidays/newyear.htm. Indiana science teacher Jerry Wilson has assembled this concise and lively page, which includes related links and activities.

San José State University. http://www.sjsu.edu/faculty/watkins/cultrev.htm. For a concise, easy-to-understand article explaining the Chinese Cultural Revolution, including photos and timeline, see Professor Thayer Watkins's link.

Things Asian. http://www.thingsasian.com. Things Asian is an online resource of Things Asian Press. Things Asian publishes three main genres: photo essays, fact files, and written articles. The site emphasizes art, culture, history, and travel.

Picture Credits

PAGE

viii: AP Photo/Frank Franklin II

2: AP Photo/POLFOTO,
Pelle Rink

3: AP Photo/Norbert Schiller

5: AP Photos/Ed Andrieski

8: AP Photo/Efrem Lukatsky

11: AP Photo/Greg Baker

13: Reuters/Alberto
Franco/Landov

14: AP Photo/Tina Fineberg

15: AP Photo/Tanya Makeyeva

17: AP Photo/Aaron Favila

30: AP Photo/Vincent Yu

32: AP Photo/Kin Cheung

34: AP Photo/Lo Sai Hung

35: AP Photo/Greg Baker

36: AP Photo/Kathy Willens

37: AP Photo/Andy Wong

39: AP Photo/Gary Chuah

40: AP Photo/Cheng Len-nan

41: AP Photo/Vincent Yu

42: AP Photo/ Richard Lam,CP

44: AP Photo/Obed Zilwa

48: AP Photo/Anat Givon

51: AP Photo/Itsuo Inouye

52: AP Photo/Atsushi Tsukada

53: Kyodo via AP Images

55: AP Photo/Kyodo News

56: AP Photo/Yonhap

57: AP Photo/Ahn Young-joon

58: AP Photo/Yun Jai-hyoung

59: AP Photo/Ng Han Guan

62: AP Photo/Aaron Favila

63: AP Photo/Jerome Favre

64: AP Photo/Richard Vogel

66: AP Photo/Hans Punz

68: dpa/Landov

69: AP Photo/Czarek Sokolowski

70: AP Photo/Alberto Estevez

71: AP Photo/Vadim Ghirda

72: AP Photo/Oleg Nikishin

74: AP Photo/Martin Ruetschi

77: EMPICS/Landov

78: Reuters/David Moir/Landov

80: AP Photo/Luis Benavides

81: AP/Photo Santiago Armas

82: AP Photo/Tim Aylen, Bahamas
Information Services

83: AP Photo/Andre Luiz Mello

84: AP Photo/Douglas Engle

85: AP Photo/Roberto Candia

93: AP Photo/CP, Richard Lam

94: AP Photo/Steven Senne

95: AP Photo/Kathy Willens

96: AP Photo/Rob Griffith

97: AP Photo/Russell McPhedran

Index

Page numbers in *italics* indicate illustrations.

A

Africa, 44–46. *See also* South Africa
    Eritrea, 44–45
    Ethiopia, 44
    Tanzania, 46
ancestors, 22, 25, 34, 58, 64, 99
Año Nuevo, 2
archipelago, 61, 99
Aruba, 82
Asakusa Sensoji Temple, Tokyo, Japan, *51*
Asia, 47–65
    Azerbaijan, 47
    China, 48–49
    India, 49
    Japan, 49–55, 62
    Korea, 56–59
    Mongolia, 59–62
    Philippines, 17, 61–62
    Taiwan, 23, 62–64
    Vietnam, 64–65
Auckland, New Zealand, *96*
"Auld Lang Syne" (Burns), 75
Australia, 96–97
Austria, 66, *66*
autocracy, 71, 99
autonomous, regions, 22–23, 99
Azerbaijan, 47

B

babies
    chubby, 29–30
    idealized, 25, 29
Babylonian Empire, 5
Bahamas, *82*, 83
balloons, 69

bamboo, 49–50
Beijing
    Temple of the Earth, *11, 35*
    Tiananmen Square, 26
birthdays
    in China, 48
    of god of wealth, 35
    of kitchen god, 48
Bituun, 60
Bolivia, 83
bonfire, 8, 49, 59, 70, 77, 99
Boston, *95*
bourgeois, 25, 99
Brazil, *83, 84*, 83–85
Buckley, Chris, 33
Buddha, 20
Buddhism, 16, 20–21, 50, 59, 99
Buddhist priests, 53
Burns, Robert, 75

C

cable cars, Chile, 86
Caesar, Julius, 9
cake
    prosperity, 30, 31
    sticky rice, 38–40
calendars
    animals corresponding on, 11–12
    around the world, 7–8
    converting dates of, 10
    Gregorian, 9–11, 49–50
    Hindu lunar, 49
    Islamic, 7–10, 47, 79
    Julian, 9
    lunar of Sumerians, 5, *5*
    Mayan, 10
    solar, 7

calendar year
    of North American Indians, 6
    origins of, 3–12
    planting and harvesting seasons,
        3–4
Canada, 42, 92, 93
Cantonese dialect, 23–24
Cape Province, South Africa, *44*
cards, 32
Caribbean. *See* Latin America
    and Caribbean
Castro, Fidel, 87
CCP. *See* Communist Party of China
Chile, 85–86
China, 48–49. *See also* People's Republic
    of China; Republic of China;
    Traditional Chinese Medicine
    Beijing, 11, 26
    birthdays in, 48
    Cantonese dialect, 23–24
Chinatown, New York City, *36*
Chinatown, Vancouver, *42*
Chinese calendar, 11–12
Chinese New Year, 11, 19–41
    cards, 32
    chubby babies, 29–30
    cleaning homes for, 27
    customs, 27–40
    decorations, 28
    dumplings, 31
    family relationships on, 34
    festivities, 35–38
    fireworks, 38
    history of, 22–27
    lanterns, 38–40
    lucky foods, 30–31
    origins, 19
    parade, Vancouver, Canada,
        42, 92, 93
    prosperity cake, 30, 31
    puns, 29
    rituals of, 35
    round foods, 31–32
    special poems for, 27–28
    sticky rice cakes, 38–40
    winter storm of 2008, 33
Chun Jie (Spring Festival), 19

*chun lian (*spring couplet), 27
cleaning homes, 27
Colombia, *80*
communist, 24–25, 28, 56,
    59, 72–73, 87, 99
Communist Party of China (CCP), 24–25
Confucianism, 22
Constitution Square, Athens, 66
Copenhagen, Denmark, 2
couplet, 27–28, 99
crescendo, 59, 99
Cuba, 86–87
Cultural Revolution, 25–26
cut paper decorations and posters, 28
Cyprus, 91
Czech Republic, 67

D

dance
    with bottles, 89
    dragon, 48
    mask, 58
danza (dancing with bottles on head), 89
Daodejing (Lao Tzu), 21
Daoism, 20–21
decorations, 28
Denmark, 2, 67
dictator, 9, 56, 87, 89, 99
dragon dance, 36, 38, 48
dragons, 35–38
dumplings, 31, 32

E

Ecuadoreans, *13*, *81*
Edo period, Japan, 52
Egypt, *3*
Ekeko, god of abundance, 83
Elephant Chess, 35
end-of-the-year bell, 53
England, 75–76
English, Jane, 21
Eritrea, 44–45
Ethiopia, 44
Europe, 66–78
    Austria, 66
    Czech Republic, 67

Denmark, *2*, 67
France, 67–68
Germany, 68–69
Italy, 68–69
Lithuania, 68
Poland, 68–69
Portugal, 23, 70
Romania, 70–71
Russia, 71–73
Spain, 73–74
Switzerland, 74–75

F

family relationships, 34
Feng, Gia-Fu, 21
fireworks, *28*, *41*, *55*, *56*, 66,
    68, 83, *85*, 86, 97
first-footer tradition, 76
First Nations, 6
First Night Parade, Boston, 94
fish, 31
food
    lucky, 30–31
    round, 31–32, *32*
France, 67–68

G

Gaspar Rodríguez de Francia, José, 89
Gautama Buddha, 20
Gautama, Siddhartha, 20
Germany, 68, *68*
glutinous rice, 39, 99
goddess of sea, 84–85
god of abundance, 83
grapes, 79
Greece, 66
Greenland, 92–93, 94. *See also* Denmark
Gregorian calendar, 9–11, 49–50
Gregorian New Year, 13–18
Gregory XIII (Pope), 9
Guatemala, 88–89

H

Haile Selassi, 44
Hindu, 9, 47, 49, 99

Hindu lunar calendar, 49
Ho Chi Minh City, Vietnam, *64*
Hogmonay festival, Scotland,
    77–78
Hong Kong, 23, *30*, *34*, 38, 41, *48*
Hourglass Park, Jeongdongjin, 57
Huan-chang, Lee, 28
hui chun (returning to spring), 27

I

India, 49
International Date Line, 16
Ireland, 75
Islam, 72, 91, 100
Islamic calendar, 7–10, 47, 79
Italy, 68–69

J

Jade Emperor, 21
Jamaica, 87–88
January, meaning of, 15
Japan, 49–55, *55*
Jeongdongjin, 57
joya no kane (end-of-the-year bell),
    53
Julian calendar, 9
Junkanoo group, Nassau,
    Bahamas, 82

K

kadomatsu, 50, 52
Kangnyoung Mask Dance, *58*
Khan, Genghis, 59
Kiev, Ukraine, 8
Kiribati, 98
kitchen god, 48, 65
Korea, 56–59
Kuala Lumpur, Malaysia, *37*
Kyoto, *53*

L

language, tonal, 23
Lantern Festival, 40, 64
lanterns, 38–40, 51, 64
Lao Tzu, 21

Latin America and Caribbean, 79–90
    Aruba, 82
    Bahamas, 82, 83
    Bolivia, 83
    Brazil, 83–85
    Chile, 85–86
    Cuba, 86–87
    Guatemala, 88–89
    Jamaica, 87–88
    Mexico, 88–89
    Paraguay, 89–90
lettuce wraps, 30
line of succession, 100
Lithuania, 68
Logan, Christopher, 28
luck
    foods for, 30–31
    red for, 26
lunar, 100. *See also* solilunar
    calendars of Sumerians, 5
    Hindu, 49

M

Macau, 23
Malaysia, *37, 39*
Mandarin dialect, 23–24
Manila, Philippines, *17, 62*
Mao Zedong, 25
Mayan calendar, 10
Mayan peoples, 88
Mexico, 88–89
Middle East, 91
mistletoe, 67–68
moda amarilla (yellow fashion), 80
monarch, 100
Mongolia, 59–62
moon phases, 4–6
moratorium, 67, 100
Moscow, *15, 72*
Mount Kilimanjaro, 46
municipalities, 22, 100

N

New Year. *See also* Chinese New Year
    greetings around the world, 18, 19
    Gregorian, 13–18

observances, 9
    traditions of, 16
New York City, 14, 36, 93–94, 95
New Zealand, 96
North America, 92–95
    Canada, 42, 92, 93
    Greenland, 92–93, 94
    United States, 94–95
North American Indians, 6–7

O

Oceania, 96–98
    Australia, 96–97
    Kiribati, 98
    Tonga, 98
old year, getting rid of, 81–82
"Old Year's Burn," 13
Ong Dao (kitchen god), 65
Orthodox Monastery of Caves,
    Kiev, Ukraine, 8
otoso (herbal drink), 54–55

P

paper cutter, 28
Paraguay, 89–90
People's Republic of China
    (PRC), *11*, 23, 28, 100
Philippines, 17, 61–62, *61*
pine trees, 49–50
Ping-huang, Chang, 28
plum trees, 49–50
poems, 27–28
Poland, 69, *69*
Portugal, 23, 70
propaganda, 25, 100
prosperity cake, 30, 31
puns, 29

Q

Quiller-Couch, Arthur Thomas, 75

R

Ramadan, 7
Red Guard, 25–26
Red Square, Moscow, *15*

Republic of China (ROC), 23
Republic of China Calligraphy
    Association, 28
resolution, 15, 16, 44, 49, 52, 73, 92, 100
Romania, 70–71, *71*
round foods, 31–32
Royal Society for Prevention and
    Cruelty to Animals, 96
Russia, 71–73, *72*

S

Saint Sylvester feast day, 66, 68
Santiago, Chile, *85*
SARS. *See* Special administrative
    Regions
Scotland, 76–78, *77*, *78*
seasons, 3–4
Seoul, South Korea, *56*, *58*
shimenawa, *52*
Shinto, 50, 100
Shogatsu, 2
shortbread, 16, 76, 100
Silvesterchlaeuse, 74
Sky Tower, Aukland, New Zealand, 96
solar, 100
    -based way to track time, 3–4
    calendars, 7
solilunar, 7, 8, 100
Sor, 61
Sosigenes, 9
South Africa, 44, 45–46
South Korea, 56, 57, *57*, 58
Spain, *70*, 73–74
special administrative regions (SARs), 22
Spring Festival, 19
Star Wars, 60
steel drums, 87, 88
sticky rice cakes, 38–40
Sumerians, 5
Switzerland, 74, 74–75
Sydney Harbor Bridge, *97*
Sylvesterabend, 66

T

Taipei, Taiwan, *63*
Taiwan, 23, *40*, 62–64

Tanzania, 46
TCM. *See* Traditional Chinese
    Medicine
temperate, 100
Temple of Earth fair, Beijing, 11, 35
Temple of the Earth, 11, 35
Tet, 64–65
Tiananmen Square, 26
time
    moon phases defining, 4–6
    solar-based way to track, 3–4
Times Square, New York City,
    viii, *14*, *94*, 94–95
Tokyo, 51, 52
Tonga, 98
Traditional Chinese Medicine (TCM), 24
tropical, 100
Tsagaan Tsar (white month), 60
Turkey, 91
typhoon, 100

U

Ukraine, *8*
Ulaanbaator, Mongolia, 59, *59*
underwear, colored, 80
Union of Socialist Soviet
    Republics (USSR), 72
United Kingdom, 23
    England, 75–76
    Ireland, 75
    Scotland, 76–78
    United Kingdom, 75
United States, 14, 94–95
USSR. *See* Union of Socialist
    Soviet Republics

V

Vancouver, Canada, *93*
Vatican City, 69
Victoria Harbor, Hong Kong, 38, *41*
Vietnam, 64–65

W

Wajxaqib' B'at'z, 88
Walker, John, 10

Wen Jibao, 33
white month, 60
Wu, Grace, 32

Y

Year of the Rat, 12
yellow fashion, 80

Yemajá, goddess of sea, 84–85
yin and yang, 20–21

Z

Zao Jun (kitchen god), 48
Zojoji Temple, Tokyo, *52*

About the Author

Elizabeth A. Dice has been a writer, editor, and project manager for more than 25 years, working in educational publishing for 10 of those years. She has also taught English, Spanish, ESL, graphic design, and calligraphy. Elizabeth received a B.A. in English from Smith College and an M.A. in English from Michigan State University.